INSIGHT COMPACT GUIDES

Insight Compact Guide: Amsterdam unveils the elegance – tidy and tousled at the same time – of this canal-laced city, once the centre of a global empire and now perhaps Europe's most tolerant and embracingly pleasurable city.

This is just one title in *Apa Publications'* new series of pocket-sized, easy-to-use guidebooks intended for the independent-minded traveller. Based on an established, award-winning formula pioneered in Germany, *Insight Compact Guides* pride themselves on being up-to-date and authoritative. They are in essence mini travel encyclopedias, designed to be comprehensive yet portable, both readable and reliable.

Star Attractions

An instant reference to some of Amsterdam's most popular tourist attractions to help you on your way.

Koninklijk Palace p 22

Nieuwe Kerk p 23

Keizersgracht p 24

Catholic Church Begijnhof p27

Westerkerk p 38

Anne Frank House p 39

Concertgebouw p 42

Rijksmuseum p 43

Utrecht Cathedral Cloister p 48

AMSTERDAM

Introduction

Places

Culture

Leisure

Practical Information

13
688

Amsterdam – The Intimate City

Amsterdam, which was formerly known as Amstelredam (the Romans called it *Amstelodamum*), is the most popular destination for visitors to The Netherlands. In many respects the city has the atmosphere of a capital city, but it is in fact only the nominal capital. The seat of government is in The Hague and the Royal family is only occasionally in residence at the Royal Palace on Dam Square.

Amsterdam has a much more intimate character than most great European cities. This is best reflected in the narrow, bustling streets of the old town, where much of the population still goes about its business. The city is famed for its centuries-old canals, and one of the nicest ways of getting to know the place is indeed from the water, on one of the many canal cruise boats. As you travel from bridge to bridge, there are constant reminders of the glorious past. Historic churches and towers rise above fine patrician houses and warehouses. With their distinctive gables and brick facades, these are the enduring legacy of Amsterdam's Golden Age, when, in the 17th century, the city emerged as a major trading metropolis. Merchant ships from Amsterdam sailed not only to the Baltic and the Mediterranean but also plied the long sea route to the East Indies and established colonies as far afield as South America and southern Africa. This was the time when the Dutch cartographers became famous. Their maps were regarded as the most accurate and most beautiful and are still highly praised today. Increasing prosperity saw the city blossom as a city of culture and the arts. That legacy, too, is preserved today in some of the finest museums in the world.

The romantic image of Amsterdam – of barrel organs, carillons, canals and houseboats – is but one aspect of the city. Just as much a hallmark is the atmosphere of freedom and tolerance. Born out of the city's permanent link with the world beyond, in modern times it has attracted numerous people seeking an alternative lifestyle. But Amsterdam is also confronted by the attendant problems of any modern metropolis, particularly where space is at a premium. Environmental polution, traffic congestion and housing shortages are matters for which lasting solutions still have to be found.

Geography and geology

Amsterdam's approximate latitude is 52°50'N and its longitude is 4°53'E, standing on the north and south bank of the IJ which links the southern end of the huge IJsselmeer lake and the North Sea. The land is marshy, with clay and sandy soil, a fact which has always posed major problems for the construction industry. Long piles have

Opposite: View towards Dam Square

Busy narrow streets

Cruise boat by Centraal Station

Houseboat on the Singel

to be driven deep into the ground; the bigger the project the deeper they have to go. As a rule, digging and securing the foundations accounts for one third of building costs. A few decades ago, only tree trunks could be used as supporting piles, but now reinforced concrete is hammered into the ground with mechanical pile-drivers.

Commerce and industry

The dominant role that Amsterdam occupied in world trade during the 17th and 18th centuries has long disappeared. Its significance as the world's warehouse has also waned but there are some industries in which Amsterdam is still the world leader. Before World War II, the Amsterdam tea and tobacco auctions attracted buyers from all the leading trading nations as a consequence of their links with the Dutch East Indies, now Indonesia. Rubber is also a commodity which is traded on the exchange in considerable quantities, even though it is no longer imported. Sugar is exported around the world, there is trade in cotton, pepper and spices. Other important merchandise includes oil, fats, cereals, cocoa, citrus fruits, skins, leather, furs and diamonds.

Diamond polishing

The Dutch banking world is based in Amsterdam. As well as the country's central bank De Nederlandse Bank, the biggest private bank, the Algemene Bank Nederland, also has its headquarters in the city. In addition many smaller banks, credit companies, finance houses and the branches of foreign banks are situated in Amsterdam. It has become an important international exchange and finance centre. The Netherlands has been a member of the European Community since 1958.

Stock Exchange detail

The Amsterdam Stock Exchange also has an important international role. It handles more share dealings than most European stock exchanges. The currency market too has a significant part to play in financial circles. Many Dutch and foreign insurance companies have branches in Amsterdam as well as a number of property agencies.

Amsterdam's industries have traditionally been linked with shipping and the processing of imported products. After the Noordzee canal was opened, many new companies moved there and the area now has a broad and diverse industrial base. Factories have located to the north and south of the IJ, and metalworking and chemicals are well established.

Linen manufacture and ready-to-wear clothing employ many local people, as do an assortment of chocolate and cigarette factories and some large breweries. The printing and publishing industry is of great importance, with 350 printing works and 107 publishers located in the region.

Amsterdam's industry

Much of Amsterdam's industry is inextricably linked to the vast conglomeration of manufacturing plants in the areas alongside the Noordzee canal. Much of the space on the industrial estates in the south and west of Amsterdam is occupied by Dutch firms which have relocated there from the inner city areas. The chemical and petrochemical industries are coming under close scrutiny from a public which is increasingly aware of the threat to the environment that such companies pose.

Some of the important research establishments in the area include the Shell laboratory, the National Aeronautics laboratory, the Institute of Nuclear Physics and the Mathematical Centre.

Amsterdam port

The port of Amsterdam is the second biggest port in Holland after Rotterdam and its former function was always as a centre for imports and warehousing. Although it is still important in this capacity, it is now mainly an import and export terminal serving the Dutch and German hinterland. Amsterdam's importance as an industrial port is continuing to grow.

Boat on the Zuider Zee

Until 1824, all shipping had to pass through the Zuider Zee. In the course of time, the shipping channels silted up, so that seafaring vessels needed to be carried over the sandbanks by so-called 'camels'. Even the port entrance was closed off mechanically.

Subsequently, the Groot Noordhollandsch canal was dug from the IJ to the northernmost tip of Holland, but it did not adequately meet the expectations of the Amsterdam shipping companies, so in 1862 work began on the east–west Noordzee canal, which opened in 1876. It was only then that Amsterdam could really call itself a sea port. Rhine traffic had used the Merwede canal until 1952, even though it had proved inadequate ever since its opening in 1892. Succeeded by the Amsterdam–Rhine canal, it too has now to adapt to the changing demands of river and canal transport.

Sea lock and ships at Ijmuiden

The port of Amsterdam consists of an older section in the east with rectangular islands where the offices of the main shipping companies are situated. The rest of the port complex is mainly involved with handling goods in bulk. When the outer harbour at IJmuiden has been extended, ships with a gross registered tonnage of up to 80,000, possibly even 100,000, will be able to travel 20km (13 miles) upstream, although the railway bridge at Hem must first be replaced by a tunnel. Once the canal has been widened to 170m (500ft) and dredged to a depth of 15.5m (48ft), the canal will be the widest and deepest one in the world.

The harbour basin covers about 1,200ha (3,000 acres). Amsterdam is important as a port for Rhine traffic. The berths for Rhine barges are situated where the Amsterdam–Rhine canal joins the IJ.

Getting to work

Population

Of the estimated 939,000 inhabitants of Amsterdam, 150,000 come from other countries. Accommodation in the city is made up of around 300,000 houses with a further 1,100 houseboats.

Seven percent of the working population of the Netherlands is employed in Amsterdam, but do not all live there. As in most other major European cities, natives of Amsterdam have shunned the busy inner city area and have chosen to live in suburban centres, such as Amstelveen, where wide roads and good public transport make travelling a less irksome pastime than in the bustling narrow streets and heavy traffic of the centre. Around 70,000 commuters are ferried backwards and forwards from their dormitory towns and commuter belts by car, bus and train.

Growing population

Population pressures

The geology around Amsterdam does not permit the construction of high-rise flats, which is so often the response of urban authorities to a burgeoning population. In retrospect this has proved to be no bad thing, although it has led to a proliferation of offices and factories on the outskirts of the city, a development which has been to the detriment of suburban life styles. The movement of population away from the city centre has also had its consequences. At the end of the 19th century over 300,000 people lived in the old town; now that number has dwindled to about 75,000. However, there has been a noticeable reversal in this trend in recent years. Initially, young academics and artists rediscovered the old gabled houses, but then banks and multi-national companies realised the

Egelantiersgracht

advantages that accrued from having a renovated property and a prestigious address beside one of the famous canals.

Transportation

The Amsterdam conurbation is one of the most congested parts of Holland. Main railway lines from Haarlem, Zaandam, Hilversum and Utrecht converge on the central station, which was built on an artificial island. The rail network then extends across the whole country. Some 10 million passengers use the Amsterdam stations each year.

Fast roads and motorways lead off in all directions. Both the E25 motorway to Genoa and the E35 to Hamburg start in Amsterdam. The E19/E22 from Paris to Bremen via Groningen passes close to the city. The traffic flow between the city centre and the outlying areas north of the IJ and the Noordzee canal is shared between the Schellingwoude bridge over the outer IJ, the Coen Tunnel, opened in 1966, and the IJ tunnel, completed in 1968. The suburbs to the south, the port and the industrial areas south of the Noordzee canal are now linked by the Hem tunnel with the Zaanland on the opposite side.

City tram

Cycle lane

Amsterdam's international airport at Schiphol is on the E19 motorway to The Hague and Rotterdam and, as Holland's main airport, it serves 120 different cities throughout the world. Around 16 million passengers pass through the terminals each year.

The city transport services run 16 tram routes with about 240 trams, 30 bus routes with 424 buses, and two underground lines. About 95,000 people use the public transport network each day. The 23.4km (15 miles) of existing underground lines have cost the city authorities 1 billion guilders. Because of the high cost, there are not likely to be any more lines for the time being and it is safe to assume that the bicycle will continue to be the most important form of transport for short distances. It is reckoned that, at the moment, there are over 550,000 bicycles in Amsterdam, ridden by young and old alike, with the complete confidence of people who know that the city belongs to them. Some six hundred taxis also operate within the confines of the city.

Some more statistics

The city claims to have 8,850 shops and nine markets, most of which are open every day. Amsterdam is also a city of culture with 45 museums, 12 theatres, 25 church organs, nine chiming church bells and nine barrel organs. There are almost 25,000 hotel beds available with overnight stays totalling 3.2 million each year. The city has over a thousand bridges and the waterways, which comprise of more than 100 canals, clock up a combined length of more than 100km (65 miles).

Welcome to Amsterdam

Prinsengracht images

Canals and Other Developments

Known as *grachten*, the canals were initially dug out for defensive purposes, but small boats proved very useful as a means of transport and in the 17th century the network was extended. There are now over 100 canals, some of which have acquired world-wide fame. The canals are still used to transport goods around the inner city area and a special flat-bottomed, open barge is used.

The canals are linked to the IJ and every night sluice gates are opened and a measured flow of fresh water is allowed into the canal system. Any overflow passes into the Noordzee canal, thereby ensuring that the water level remains constant. It is important that the millions of tree trunks which support the buildings of Amsterdam stay underwater so that they do not decay.

Phase 1 (up to 1612)

The oldest part of the city lies on both banks of the Amstel but is protected from the IJ by a dam. It is not certain when this dam was built, but documents have shown that it was the construction of this protective barrier which led to the founding of the town in 1275. Amsterdam celebrated its 700th anniversary in 1975.

The town's first port was established along the waterway which linked the Amstel and the IJ (now the Damrak). Warmoestraat, Nes and Zeedijk fall within the old town area and the Oude Kerk (Old Church) was built in the old town. The Oude- and Nieuwezijds Voorburgwal (Old and New Town canals) were dug in 1342, forming the first defensive barrier for the town. The Spui and Grimburgwal linked the two canals.

By the end of the 15th century the rapidly growing town had overflowed beyond its defensive ramparts. The boundary ran along Singel, Geldersekade and Kloveniersburgwal and the first stone town walls were built. The line was drawn further out in 1585 to encompass the shipyards and warehouses. The outer ring of walls was reinforced with stronger bastions. The Jewish quarter in the north-east of the old town was also established at around that time. The fourth enlargement in 1593 extended the boundaries of the town as far as the Blauwbrug, Amstelstraat and Reguliersdwarstraat.

Phase 2 (from 1612)

The ring of canals comprising the Herengracht, Keizersgracht and Prinsengracht was built at the beginning of the 17th century, the Golden Age of the Netherlands. The driving force behind the scheme was the mayor of Amsterdam, Frans Hendrickszoon Oetgens, but he was supported by city carpenter-in-chief Hendrik Straets and surveyor Lucas Dakkerts. It is assumed that Hendrik de Keyser, later to become one of the town's leading architects, also made an important contribution at the planning stage. On 16 April 1610, the plans were approved by Amsterdam's council, and work began in 1612.

Herengracht Canal

The project, known as the Three Canal Plan, was too big to be completed in one stage. First Herengracht was created by widenening the narrow canal behind the old town wall, which had to be demolished. Keizersgracht and Prinsengracht followed and the three canals ended at what is now Leidsegracht. The semi-circular network was extended by the addition of some smaller canals and streets. The Singel was intended to be the outer limit of the canal ring but by the end of the century, the rapid improvement in Amsterdam's economic fortunes meant that more canals had to be dug on the east side of the Amstel: Nieuwe Herengracht, Nieuwe Keizersgracht and Nieuwe Prinsengracht.

The concentric rings of canals were linked by a number of narrow radial canals and roads which once led to the town gates. The resulting criss-cross network of canals created about 90 small islands linked by over 400 stone bridges, known as *sluizen* or sluices. Between the waterways there was enough land to build spacious houses with gardens. The construction of this system of canals was one of the biggest building projects ever undertaken by the Dutch people. The work had to be done by hand, shovel and wheelbarrow, although much of the labour was supplied cheaply as huge numbers of convicts were drafted in to work on the canals.

Canal-side garden

Phase 3 (18th and 19th centuries)

The new semi-circular lay-out provided plenty of room for the city to develop, especially as the local economy

Housing estate plans

suffered during the 18th century. It was not until the second half of the 19th century, when the economic situation improved and the population grew, that new residential districts were needed, mainly outside the Singelgracht, but also in the south, west and east of the city: De Pijp, Kinker- and Staatsliedenbuurt, Dapperbuurt and Indische Buurt. At the time, the new homes represented a tremendous improvement in the living conditions of the people, but nowadays these cheerless parts of the city pose serious problems as the buildings have started to decay. Plans to redevelop the areas have come up against organised resistance by the local people.

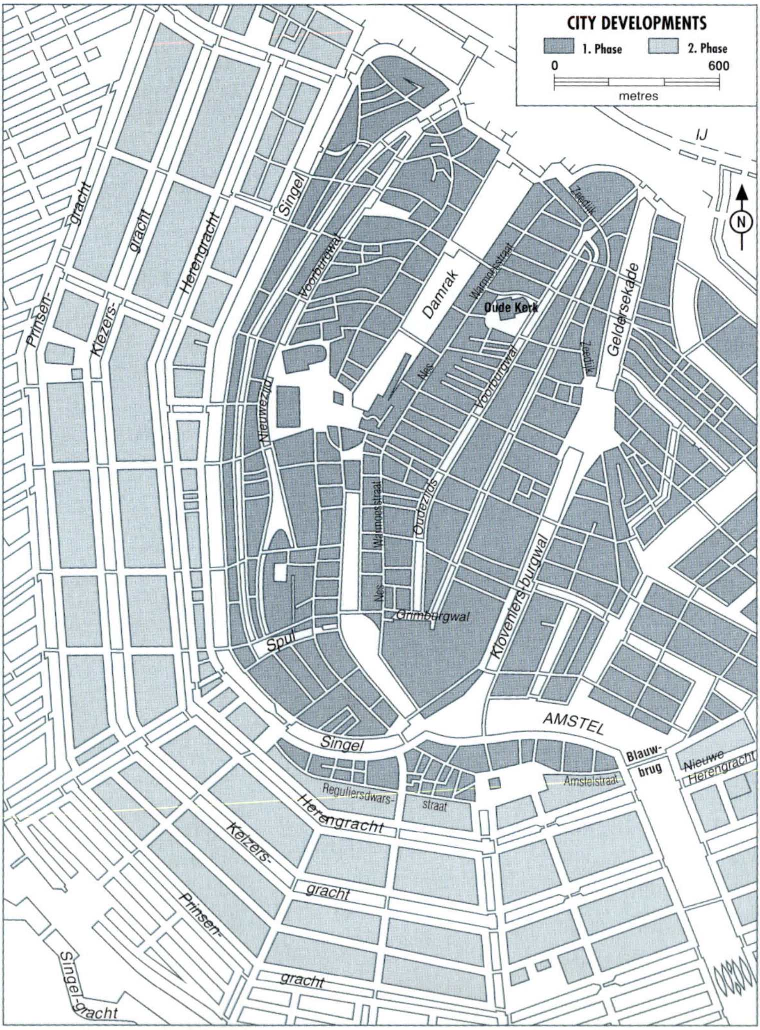

The 19th century also saw the development of the area around Sarphatistraat with the Amstel Hotel and the People's Palace, which was destroyed by fire in 1929. The Concertgebouw and Rijksmuseum districts also grew up at the end of the last century and were settled mainly by the well-to-do, who built solid homes for themselves. The arrival of the railway in the port area placed restrictions on how the city was to develop and the architectural style and location of the main station (Centraal Station) aroused considerable criticism from the local population.

The Concertgebouw

Phase 4 (20th century)

Immediately after World War I, Hendrik Pieter Berlage's South Plan, which envisaged residential areas for the masses, was carried out, but the Amsterdam School of architects opposed Berlage's rigid functionality. Their approach was to hide structural components behind an ornate facade. The influence of English architects who favoured a blend of town and country led to the garden suburbs of Watergraafsmeer and Oostzaan. During the 1920s and 30s the smart Apollolaan estate was built.

In the Amsterdam of the 19th and early 20th centuries, planners and architects preferred long lines of streets with uniform, brick-built houses, but in the post-Berlage era, there has been a deliberate move towards diversity. These principles have been incorporated throughout the modern Amsterdam suburbs of Bos en Lommer, Slotermeer, Slotervart, Geuzenfeld, Osdorp, Westlandgracht and Overtoomseveld in the west and Buitenveldert and Bijlmermeer in the south. The IJ tunnel and the Schellingwouder Bridge in the east have freed north Amsterdam from its traditional isolation and here too a number of residential areas have been established. Town planners are anticipating that Amsterdam's population will rise to one million by the end of the century.

Preservation work

Town preservation

Since World War II, over 600 of the old buildings inside the canal ring have had to be demolished. Day after day from 6am until midnight, constant vibration from cars and lorries has damaged the foundations, walls, roofs and facades. Pumping out water from the foundations of new buildings has led to fluctuations in the underground water levels, the old piles have been exposed and this has led to subsidence.

There has been pressure for a rescue plan to be implemented. Several organisations such as the Friends of Diogenes and Amstelodamum have been founded, all with one objective: the preservation of the city's historic buildings. But the campaign is unlikely to be successful unless huge sums of money are forthcoming.

Based in an old ferry house by the Amstel, the Diogenes Foundation has long sought to protect Amsterdam's bricks and mortar. Its aim is to make Amsterdam's historic old houses available to artists. In 1962 the foundation invested 4,000 guilders in a small house in the Jordaan district of the city. The money had been donated by an artists' association called Arti et Amicitiae, and by a judge. Now Diogenes owns over 100 premises in the old town, which are leased to artists of every kind.

In Jordaan, behind a door overgrown with ivy, an empty 17th-century almshouse was discovered; now it is home to artists and students who have painted the rooms in the original blue and pink colour scheme.

Potter at work

Historic canal houses

Property

Historic canal houses are favourites with the property market. An agency known as the Maatschappij Stadtherstel, founded by the brewer Jonkheer Six van Hillegom, buys 17th- and 18th-century houses, restores them with public grants of 70 percent and then sells each storey separately to new romantics – a sort of Rousseau in reverse: back to the city.

Floating homes

The houseboats on the canals can initially give an impression of idyllic serenity – the perfect life style – but in fact they have become a serious problem for the authorities. It is estimated that 10,000 people live in the 2,500 barges moored on the canal banks. Although there are approved 'water villas' on the canals, the main objection to the flotilla of houseboats has to do with the untreated effluent which flows directly into the canal water.

Houseboat on the Singel

Durgerdam

The IJ

The IJ (pronounced 'eye') used to be an arm of the Zuider Zee, and when it was at its biggest in the Middle Ages, it stretched across the province of Noord-Holland as far as the North Sea dunes between Haarlem and Beverwijk. It has been in retreat ever since, much of the land has been reclaimed and it is now only 10km (7 miles) long: from Schellingwoude/Durgerdam in the east to Tuindoorp-Oostzaan in the west. The IJ forms the central port area for Amsterdam and in 1895 the main station was built on a 2-km (1 ¼-mile strip of land reclaimed from the river. On the opposite bank are the locks to the entrance of the Noordhollandsch canal, the waterway to Den Helder. At the Schellingwoude Bridge, the IJ is kept at bay by the Oranje locks. The Amsterdam port area is often known as the Afgesloten-IJ (closed IJ) in contrast to Buiten-IJ (outer IJ), which links with the old Zuider Zee further north and is usually known as the IJsselmeer.

Zuider Zee (IJsselmeer)

Many old maps still contain references to the Zuider Zee, but plans were initially laid in 1918 to cut it off from the North Sea by a barrage between the north Dutch and Friesian mainland. Work did not begin until 1927 and it was not completed until 1932. The rivers feeding the bay have turned it into a huge freshwater lake. The biggest tributary is the IJssel, the northern arm of the Rhine delta. The Dutch word *zee* means sea, and as it was no longer a sea the name Zuider Zee seemed inappropriate. As the IJssel contributed most to the new lake, IJsselmeer (IJssel lake) was chosen.

Marken, Zuider Zee

In 1927 work started on draining large areas of land adjacent to the Zuider Zee. This reclaimed land is known as *polder*. The first section to be reclaimed was the tip of the Noord-Holland province known as Wieringermeer. In 1930 the Wieringermeer *polder* was opened, followed by the Nordoost *polder* (1935–42). To reclaim the land, an encircling dam is built with the aid of special barges and then water is pumped out of the enclosed area. The Oostflevoland *polder* was formed in this way between 1950 and 1957. Zuidflevoland was cleared of water in 1968 and the first settlements were established in 1974. The Muiden *polders* near Amsterdam have provided the city authorities with an opportunity to tackle some of the housing shortage problems. The Markerwaard encircling dam has now been completed and the Marken Islands are now part of the mainland. Once the whole project has been completed, new land to the north of Amsterdam will be available for housing developments, although the residents of the small townships nearby are set to resist further encroachment. Many people wish to retain the views over the water and prevent further building. Even agricultural use of the land was not considered profitable. Plans to build a new airport in the Markerwaard have been shelved for the time being.

Polder Museum

The full story of the *polders* and the social upheaval is documented in the Zuider Zee Museum at Enkhuizen, to the north of Amsterdam.

In the Nieuw Land Information Centre at Lelystad (Oostflevoland), there is an exhibition on the Zuider Zee project which uses audiovisual presentations. In Ketelhaven (Flevoland), to the east of Amsterdam, there is an interesting museum of maritime archaeology with a display recounting the history of the old Zuider Zee.

If you are interested in the *polders* and want to see something of the countryside outside Amsterdam, take a trip along the old Zuider Zee dyke roads and enjoy one of Holland's finest landscapes (*see Excursion 3*).

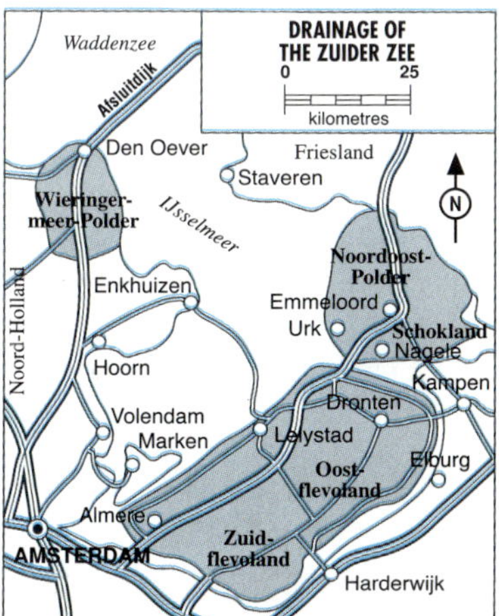

Historical Highlights

13th century Amsterdam is founded beside a dam on the River Amstel. The dam, which is built on the marshy land at the mouth of the river, creates a natural harbour in the southwest corner of the Zuider Zee (the IJ): Amstelredam.

The local population of merchants and sailors are granted customs concessions by Floris V, the Count of Holland. The town quickly becomes a prosperous port.

c 1300 Amsterdam receives its city charter from Guy van Avesnes (Henegouwen).

c 1317 Count Willem III of Holland takes control of the city from the bishops of Utrecht.

After 1323 The city benefits economically from beer imports from Hamburg. In 1367, Amsterdam joins the Cologne Confederation and the city soon becomes an important trading centre for grain between the Baltic and Flanders.

c 1395 The first town hall is built on the site of the Royal Palace in Dam Square. Power in Amsterdam rests with the merchant families, who lay the foundations for an empire which eventually encompasses the whole world.

15th century Amsterdam is described as the 'granary of the northern Netherlands'. The city's fame derives from a miracle. According to the legend a dying man refused to take the last rites. The wafer that he was offered was thrown into the fire, but was not consumed by the flames. In 1347 a chapel was built in Kalverstraat on the site of this miracle. Emperor Maximilian I visits the chapel on returning from a pilgrimage and is cured of a fatal disease. He thanks the people of Amsterdam by granting them the right to include his crown on the city's coat of arms.

1421 Amsterdam is destroyed by a great fire. Reconstruction takes at least four years.

1481 Mounds and palisades are replaced by a stone wall. Some of the remains are St Anthony's Gate (the Waag), the Schreierstoren and the Munttoren. Amsterdam becomes the largest town in the northern Netherlands.

1567 Amsterdam is occupied by the Duke of Alba's Spanish troops. The followers of the Reformation are persecuted, but the Spanish king, Philip II, loses his influence over the rebellious Netherlands. Amsterdam, which had until 1578 been loyal to the king, is reconciled with the United Provinces. It is decreed that no one may be persecuted for their religious beliefs.

1585 The fall of Antwerp and the blockade of the Schelde river sends many Flemish merchants to Amsterdam for safety. They are followed by exiled Portuguese Jews, and many refugees from all over Europe head for Amsterdam and safety. Their arrival enriches the city's intellectual and cultural life. In addition, the commercial links that the refugees bring with them create opportunities for Amsterdam merchants, offering markets as far afield as Russia and the Near East. At the end of the 16th century, Amsterdam benefits from another period of prosperity.

1595 A consortium of Amsterdam businessmen finance the first trip to India under Cornelis de Houtman. The East India Company and West Indies Company are founded, bringing untold wealth to the city.

1609 Amsterdam has trading links with almost 700 ports. So many different currencies are circulating in the city that the authorities set up the world's first foreign exchange. All currencies in circulation are weighed there and registered. Merchants are allowed to deposit their cash there and in 1611 the first Stocks and Commodities Exchange is established in the city.

1612 On the initiative of the city's mayor, Frans Hendrickszoon Oetgens, construction of the three famous canals begins. Merchant ships may now sail into the heart of the city.

Amsterdam becomes established as a cultural centre. In 1632, the Athenaeum Illustre is founded here (from 1877 it is known as the University of Amsterdam). The city now has well over 100,000 inhabitants.

1631 Rembrandt van Rijn decides to live and work in Amsterdam.

1642 Rembrandt paints his masterpiece *The Night Watch* (now in the Rijksmuseum).

1648 Construction of the new Town Hall in Dam Square commences, in the shadow of the New Church. Amsterdam is at the pinnacle of its economic strength and is recognised as the financial, trading and cultural centre of the world. The city exerts a considerable amount of political influence internationally, lending money to both kings and emperors. Jacob van Campen designs the palatial town hall (now the Royal Palace) on Dam Square.

1652–4 The first war with England leads to a serious loss of trade. Prosperity does not return until the end of the 17th century. Although immigrants pour into the city, the city's wealth is concentrated in fewer hands.

18th century Until the middle of the 18th century Amsterdam retains its position as a leading trading centre, but it gradually becomes the practice for commerce and goods to flow directly to their destination. Amsterdam loses its pre-eminence as an international warehouse. The collapse of the Amsterdam Exchange Bank in 1763 damages the credit market.

1780–4 The fourth war with England; Amsterdam loses its supremacy at sea.

1795 French troops invade the Netherlands.

1808 The Netherlands is incorporated into the French Empire. Louis Bonaparte, brother of Napoleon, elevates Amsterdam to capital of the Netherlands. He strips the city fathers of their power and installs his own court there. As a consequence of Napoleon's blockade of England, a slow but damaging economic decline sets in.

1813 Napoleon's empire collapses and William I becomes King of the Netherlands. Amsterdam retains its status as capital but The Hague becomes the seat of government.

1819–25 Amsterdam finances the construction of the Noord-Holland canal to protect its position as a port.

1840 The old ramparts are dismantled. The strict building regulations are relaxed.

1876 The opening of the Noordzee canal gives Amsterdam direct access to the North Sea and ushers in a new period of economic prosperity.

1892 The Merwede canal is opened, improving the link from the harbour to the Rhine delta and Europe's interior.

After World War I H P Berlage begins work on new residential quarters with his South Plan, Indische Buurt and Amsterdam West. Amsterdam does not escape the recession of the 1930s.

1940 On 15 May German troops occupy the city.

1941 The uprising against the army of occupation, the 'February Strike', takes place. 100,000 Amsterdam Jews, about 10 percent of the population, are deported to concentration camps. Jodenbuurt, the Jewish quarter, is left deserted.

1944 Another popular uprising against the Germans in September, 'dolle Dinsdag', results in the imposition of a blockade against the whole of the western Netherlands.

1945 On 8 May Canadian troops liberate the city.

1946 In February, Queen Wilhelmina visits Amsterdam and praises the citizens who had withstood the blockade, using the words on the city's coat of arms: heldhaftig (heroic), vastberaden (steadfast), and barmhartig (merciful).

1952 Opening of the Amsterdam–Rhine canal helps to restore normality to Amsterdam's trade with the hinterland.

1971 Work starts on Amsterdam's first underground railway, which finally opens in 1977.

1986 The new opera house, known to locals as Stopera, is opened.

1987 The Concertgebouw and its orchestra celebrate their 100th anniversary.

1992 On 4 October an Israeli Boeing 747 cargo plane crashes into a block of flats on the Bijlmermeer housing development.

1994 400th anniversary of Holland's first tulip, arriving in Amsterdam from the court of Suleiman the Magnificent in 1594.

1995 Devastating floods submerge much of the country.

Street scene, Damrak

Preceding pages: Herengracht Canal

Centraal Station

Captain of the ship

Route 1

Around Dam Square

This route through the heart of the old town begins at the **Centraal Station** ❶. Before P J H Cuypers and A L van Gendt could lay the foundation stone for Amsterdam's neo-Renaisssance main station, three artificial islands had to be constructed on 30,000 piles between the port and Prins Hendrikkade. But they also had to contend with tremendous resistance from local people who saw in the construction of this building the desecration of their city, because it blocked the view of the harbour from Dam Square. The argument was won, however, with the support of the quayside warehouse owners who urgently needed a rail link. It is worth stopping for a moment to admire the station booking hall, as the style is more in keeping with the foyer of a late 19th-century opera house.

Leave the Stationsplein and the cheerful sounds of the huge barrel organ (*see page 73*), cross the Prins Hendrikkade and walk up Amsterdam's main street, the **Damrak** ❷, named after an extension to the port which was dug in the last century. On the left are the flag-bedecked landing-stages for the sightseeing cruises (*see page 89*). To the east, the domed tower of the St Nikolaaskerk catches the eye, but it contains little of historic interest. Also on the left, just past the boats, is the **Koopmansbeurs** ❸ (Stock Exchange). Built in 1899–1903 by Hendrik Pieter Berlage in the style of the New Realists, it attracted much international attention. Nowadays it often hosts theatre groups and special art exhibitions.

Go past the small, shady Beursplein but look beyond the square for the **Effektenbeurs**, the commodities market. Conducted tours can be organised by prior arrangement (tel: 622 0527). Stretching from the Beurs to the end of the Damrak are the shop windows of city's most prestigious department store **De Bijenkorf**. The window displays are a constant source of interest to the fashion-conscious Amsterdam residents.

Dam Square ❹ used to be the city's main market square. Nowadays it is described as the 'heart of the Netherlands' with the **Nationaal Monument** as its focal point. The 22-m (72-ft) high obelisk was erected after World War II to commemorate the liberation of the city from the German occupation. Embedded in the base of the monument are 12 urns containing earth from the eleven Dutch provinces and the former colony of Indonesia. Its construction was financed by a nationwide collection and it was officially dedicated by Queen Juliana in 1956. Part of the money was raised by the symbolic sale of square centimetres of Dam Square to a generous Dutch public. The Latin inscription on the monument translates as: 'Here at the place where the heart of the fatherland lies may

Nationaal Monument

Koninklijk Paleis

the memories which the citizens carry in their hearts look upwards to God's stars'.

During the Middle Ages the square was known as *plaetse* and in the 16th century it was the site of the public weigh-house. The buildings surrounding the square have been destroyed by fire on more than one occasion. The *Paleis op de Dam*, formerly the town hall, with its slightly top-heavy proportions, dominates the square. Although built in the middle of the 17th century to replace the town hall that had burnt down, in 1808 it became the ★ **Koninklijk Paleis** ❺ (Royal Palace), when King Louis Bonaparte decided to use it as his official residence.

The design of the palace originated from Jacob van Campen but the work was in fact completed under the direction of Daniel Stalpaert. Van Campen created a building whose exterior is a Dutch interpretation of classical style. The interior is magnificent, with a wealth of reliefs, ornamentation and marble sculptures by the Flemish sculptors A Quellinus the Elder and Rombout Verhulst.

Interior views of the Koninklijk Palace

The facade is embellished with pilasters and pedimented windows. Sea gods and unicorns pay homage to the virgin of Amsterdam while three bronze figures symbolising peace, caution and justice look on. To the rear of the building in NZ Voorburgwal, Amsterdam is seen struggling against the IJ and Amstel river gods and the four continents known to man at that time. In the gable triangle are allegorical portrayals of Atlas alongside the goddesses of moderation and vigilance.

The entrance, with its open gallery and arches, is strikingly unpretentious. The palace is topped with a silver-grey dome of Bentheim sandstone housing a carillon by

the Hemony brothers. After decades of restoration work the building is now mainly used for official state receptions. It is open during Easter holidays and from the middle of June to the end of August, daily 12.30–4pm. The state rooms follow one after the other from north to south: the Treasurer's Room with a marble fireplace and ceiling paintings by Cornelis Holsteyn; the Hall of the Aldermen with paintings by Ferdinand Bol, Govert Flinck, Jan van Bronkhorst and Jacob de Wit. The Civic Hall and Council Chamber are at the heart of the palace and both are sumptuously decorated.

Adjacent to the Palace stands the reformed ★ **Nieuwe Kerk** ❻, in Late Gothic style. It is sometimes described as the Cathedral of the Netherlands, and famous Dutch admirals, including de Ruyter, van Galen, van Kinsbergen, and the poet Vondel are buried here. Furthermore it is the church where the Dutch kings and queens are crowned. The coronation of Queen Beatrix took place here on April 30 1980, following a restoration process which had lasted nearly 20 years.

Exterior and detail of Nieuwe Kerk

The church has been destroyed by fire three times and the most recent reconstruction was in 1645. Huge clustered piers support the wooden vaulting. Of special interest are the stained-glass windows in the north wall depicting the granting of the city's coat of arms by William IV. The large window in the south wall commemorates the coronation of Queen Wilhelmina in 1898. Both windows in the north aisle were installed to celebrate the fortieth year of her reign. Admiral Michael Adriaensz de Ruyter's tombstone is the work of sculptor Rombout Verhulst.

Turn right outside the Nieuwe Kerk into Gravenstraat and pass the traditional Dutch **Drie Fleschjes** taster bar. One of Amsterdam's top hotel restaurants Die Poort van Cleve is situated where Gravenstraat meets NZ Voorburgwal. At No 284, a corner house, is a first-class antiquarian bookshop.

Drie Fleschjes taster bar

Follow the narrow Molsteeg on the east side of NZ Voorburgwal across Spuistraat with its modern art galleries and through another narrow street, Torensteeg, to the oldest canal, the ★ **Singel**. On the far side of the De Torensluis bridge at No 166 is one of Amsterdam's narrowest houses. Continue south on the west side of the canal as far as Driekoningenstraat. On the corner is the so-called **Drie Koningen Huis** ❼ with the three kings following the star to Bethlehem depicted on the gable end. There is a fine view of the ★ **Westerkerk tower** (*see page 38*) through Driekoningenstraat. Driekoningenstraat ends at the junction with the **Herengracht** and the ★★ **Bartolotti Huis** ❽ on the opposite bank. This house (No 166) was probably built around 1618 by Pieter de Keyser, the son of the master builder Hendrik de Keyser. The Dutch The-

Houseboat and garden

atre Museum (*see pages 29 and 70*) is housed here and in the adjoining building.

Follow the banks of the Herengracht north as far as the first bridge, and turn left alongside the Leliegracht. Running parallel to the Herengracht is the delightful ★ **Keizersgracht**.

Together with the Singel and Herengracht, the Keizersgracht is considered the most prestigious address in Amsterdam. No 123, the **House with the Heads**, dates from 1622 and is one of the finest mansions in the city. The gable is decorated with seven helmeted heads who are taken to be Apollo, Ceres, Mars, Pallas, Bacchus and Diana. Like the Bartolotti House, this is thought to have been designed by Pieter de Keyser around 1612. The gable stone bearing the inscription 'ZDE ZIL J A Komensky' refers to the Bohemian scholar Jan Comenius who was once a guest in the house.

The House with the Heads

It is impossible to point out every detail on these magnificent buildings but it is worth looking out for some of the delightful ornamentation: the wood-panelled doors, the wrought-iron grills or cast-iron stair rails, and gable stones with carved fruit and garlands. Photographers should come well prepared as this is the ideal place to record all the different gable designs (*see page 65*).

Wrought-iron grill

The Brouwersgracht runs at right angles to the Keizersgracht and the area around the junction of these two canals is particularly picturesque. On the corner of Binnen Brouwersgracht and easily identified by the blue paving stones outside, is a marvellous example of a house with an overhanging wooden gable. For those who still have energy to spare, a stroll down one side of the Herengracht and back along the other will prove both relaxing and stimulating, but the direct route back to the old town is to follow the Brouwersgracht over the Singel on the Haarlemmersluis and then along Nieuwendijk.

Whichever route is taken, the **Dutch West India Company** building ❾ on the Herenmarkt ought not to be overlooked. Built between 1623 and 1647 it was the headquarters of the world-famous trading company. For a long time a silver hoard looted by Admiral Piet Heyn was stored in the cellar. He had relieved the Spanish of the treasure off the island of Cuba in 1628. Nowadays one of its splendid rooms is used for solemnising marriages. Most of the rooms may be visited.

After a peaceful walk alongside the canals, the **Nieuwendijk** with its bustle, bright shop signs and adverts, eager salesmen and enthusiastic shoppers may not be to everyone's taste, but the fine step gable and gable stone at No 113 is noteworthy.

It is easy to escape the crowds by turning down one of the quieter side streets – Kolksteeg or Nieuwezijds Kolk for example. In the latter is one of the old guildhalls, the Korenmeterhuisje or the corn-carriers' hall. Wander down Sint Jacobsstraat to Sint Jacobswarsstraat where a superb bell gable can be seen at No 8 or make a quick detour to Dirk van Hasselsteeg to get a better understanding of what is meant by 'building out of alignment' (for more details about this unusual style, *see page 65*).

This route ends at Dam Square, but before seeking out a café for a relaxing drink, look for the **gable stone** on the house at the corner of the Damrak and Dam Square, as there is a piece of folk-lore attached to this carving. It represents the 4th-century Bishop of Myra, Sint Nicolaas, the patron saint of all seafarers and consequently of Amsterdam. Legend has it that as well as saving sailors in distress, he once saved three children from certain death in a brine tub and thereby became the patron saint of all children as well. Over the years, it has become the custom for adults and children to shower him with presents on his birthday, 6 December. He is also believed to bring presents to children on that day, which is the traditional Christmas gift-giving day in Holland.

Every year in the middle of November, Sinterklaas (Santa Claus) arrives in town with his servants and is given a rousing welcome by the mayor. Dam Square is closed to traffic as the local people turn out to watch the procession and the mayor's reception.

In addition, an iron ring is secured to the paving stones to mark the centre of the square. Over the Christmas period it is used as a support for the city's Christmas tree – just one small example of how practical and ingenious the Dutch can be.

Dutch West India Company

Out of alignment houses

Sinterklaas gable stone

Iron ring in Dam Square

Route 2

Dam Square – Kalverstraat – ★ Begijnhof – Herengracht – Dam Square

This route can almost be seen as a continuation of the first walk, as they both cover the streets and canals in the old town centre. It starts in Dam Square, where in 1275 Count Floris V granted customs concessions to the Amstelleredammers.

Barrel organ, Kalverstraat

Parallel to the Rokin is **Kalverstraat**. In the 1960s many exclusive and unusual shops lined this street, but sadly few of them remain. Nevertheless it is still one of Amsterdam's busiest shopping streets. It is referred to in old maps dating from as long ago as 1393, when cattle merchants sold their calves (Dutch: *kalver*), goats and sheep there with a handshake. But it was not until the beginning of the 17th century that Kalverstraat developed into one of the city's smarter shopping streets and some of the original facades to the houses still provide clues to the prosperity of the shopkeepers and merchants.

Picture of Amsterdam's shooting club

The splendid Renaissance-style doorway at No 92 marks the entrance to the courtyard of the **Historisch Museum Amsterdam** ❿ (*for opening times, see page 69*), a building which was once home to the civic orphanage. Extensive restoration work was required to recreate the original splendour, typifying the prosperity that the city enjoyed in the 16th century. The glass-covered arcade contains some huge pictures of **Amsterdam's shooting club**. The museum itself consists of several smaller buildings which are clustered around spacious courtyards, cleverly providing a link between exhibits and creating a sense of continuity.

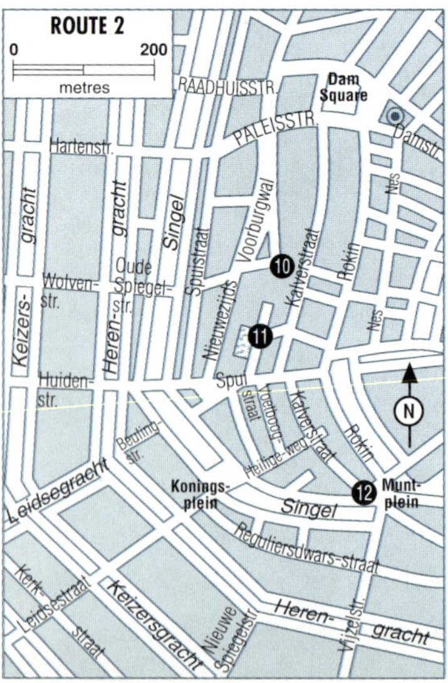

This charming corner of Amsterdam, only yards away from a busy shopping street, is an ideal place for a rainy day. On the right of the entrance under the arcades is a delightful café for weary walkers. On display in one corner is a brightly painted statue of Goliath which once stood in a late 19th-century Amsterdam garden maze. The children of a nearby orphanage used to hang their working clothes in the open gallery on the left of the entrance.

The ★ **Begijnhof** ⓫ lies at the rear of the Historisch Museum with access from Kalverstraat through the narrow Begijnensteeg passageway. This haven of tranquillity at the heart of a bustling city was founded in 1346. The Beguine nuns, pious Catholic spinsters who devoted their semi-monastic lives to serving the community, lived in three-storey houses grouped around this peace-

ful courtyard. After the Reformation, they were obliged to hand over their small Late Gothic church to the English Presbyterians. A small, concealed **Catholic church** is situated opposite. Inside can be found memorabilia relating to the Miracle of Amsterdam. The miracle, according to legend, concerns a dying man who steadfastly refused to accept the last rites. Despite all the signs of approaching death, the man recovered and enjoyed many more years of good health.

Courtyard in the Begijnhof

Window in the Catholic church

The most remarkable aspect of the miracle, however, was that the wafer which was offered to the dying man was thrown into a fire but was not consumed by the flames. On the very spot in Kalverstraat where this miracle occurred a chapel of pilgrimage was erected and survived until 1911. In March every year, a solemn procession, the *stille Omgang*, winds through the town to the hallowed spot.

The **Houten Huis** at No 34 is reckoned to be the oldest house in Amsterdam. Between Nos 37 and 38 is a door which leads through to the Spui. Note the three stones set in each wall on either side of the passage. They depict chickens, dogs and boys and refer to the fact that the Beguine nuns were not allowed to keep dogs and chickens, nor were they allowed to look after boys (Dutch: *knechte*) more than three years old.

The Houten Huis

Directly opposite on the Spui is the Maagdenhuis, formerly the orphanage for Catholic girls, which dates from the end of the 18th century.

In the middle of the busy square is Amsterdam's Little Darling, a statue known as *'t Lieverdje*. Donated to the city by a cigarette company, the boy stands, hands on hips, grinning broadly at the passers by. He represents the lively, public-spirited Amsterdam lad who is always willing to lend a hand.

The most popular attraction on the Spui is the **Hoppe**, one of the 500 or so *bruin cafés*, so-called because of the

In the Hoppe Bruin Café

browny-yellow tinge to the walls, due to an accumulation of years of tobacco smoke. Nowadays, this café, which is thought to date from 1670, is very popular with students and journalists. Most mornings at around 11am, the regulars will be drinking their first *kopje koffie* or *pilsje* standing at the counter on a floor covered in sand.

Continue through the Voetboogstraat, a narrow lane in which every house has an example of some form of gable end: pointed, step, neck, bell and moulded styles are all to be seen here.

At Heiligeweg 19 is the Rasphuis Poortje (the grating house door), which used to be the entrance to the prison. The name is derived from the fact that the prisoners had to earn their keep by grating wood chips. The carving above the door shows a woman chastising two delinquents. Underneath is another carving by Hendrik de Keyser in which the lazy pig, the sly fox, the brave lion, the cunning wolf and the greedy puma are shown cringing before the whip as they pull a cart loaded with tree-trunks.

Return to Kalverstraat and turn left towards the **Munttoren** ⓬ (Mint Towers). The towers are all that remain of the old Reguliers town gate. In 1620, Hendrik de Keyser designed the ornate, lead-covered tower, which was built above the ruined stump. The carillon plays on Tuesday and Friday at 12.30pm and 1pm.

On the other side of the arch is a bridge over the Singel, Amsterdam's oldest canal. The bridge provides a splendid view over the **floating flower market**, which stretches west as far as the Koningsplein bridge. The barges moored side by side and laden with flowers – a luxuriant display spreading in a blaze of colour – delight photographers.

A Mint Tower

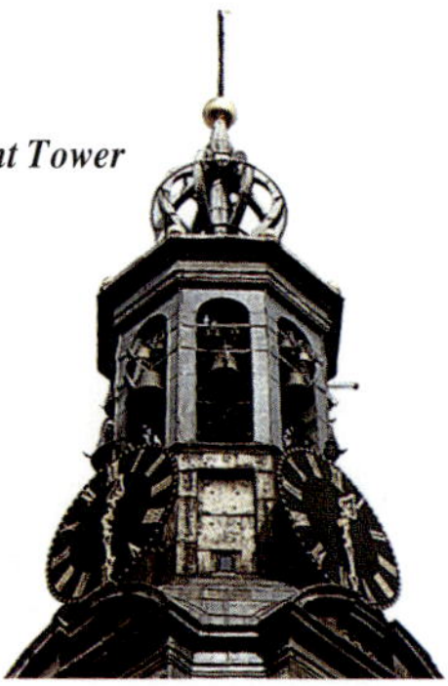

The Golden Bend

At Koningsplein turn left along Leidsestraat as far as the first bridge. Turn left again and follow the road alongside the Herengracht. This section is known to Amsterdammers as the **Golden Bend**, as it was here that the wealthiest merchants settled in the 17th century.

Lovers of antiques could well find a detour into the nearby Nieuwe Spiegelstraat and Spiegelgracht worthwhile, as this part of the city is well known for the wide choice of antique shops.

Return to the Herengracht and pay particular attention in the section between Leidsestraat and Leidsegracht, as there are a series of magnificent canal-side houses, with fine gables, in this section. Justus and Philip Vingboons are credited with the construction of these fine buildings. There is an excellent panoramic view from the bridge over the Leidsegracht. Two houses on the right-hand side (Nos 396 and 398) are known as the twin brothers while two houses opposite (Nos 427 and 429) are the twin sisters. The designs for No 402, with its monumental flight of steps, are also the work of the Vingboons brothers; at No 386 is another unusual facade, unmistakably Greek-inspired, where an imposing gable incorporates Doric and Ionic capitals

The small rooms that can be seen projecting from the front of some of the houses did have a purpose: in order to keep the kitchen spotless, domestic staff were not allowed to clean the dirty pots and pans in the kitchen, but were sent to the so-called pan-room.

The goddess of vanity and the goddess of hunting adorn the crown gable at No 376, while a little further on, the sandstone neck gables on the Kromhouthuizen (Nos 362–8) are also the work of Philip Vingboons. They were commissioned in 1662 by the shipowner Jacob Kromhout. No 366 houses the **Bijbels Museum** (*see page 69*).

It is not just the facades of these houses which are so fascinating; the magnificent gardens behind are invariably laid out in French style. The following gardens may be visited: Herengracht 166 (the **Theatre Museum**, *see pages 23 and 70*), and numbers 330, 412, 470 and 605.

To return to Dam Square, take Raadhuisstraat eastward. At the corner of NZ Voorburgwal is the former General Post Office, which has recently been converted into the Magna Plaza shopping precinct. This curious building appears to have been used by the architects for experimental purposes since as many as four different styles can be detected. Look north towards the Nieuwe Kerk and directly in front are the foundations for its church tower. When the Koninklijk Paleis was under construction, workers were taken off other projects and the church tower was never finished. Pass behind the Nieuwe Kerk and Dam Square is opposite.

Plastic flowers for sale

Theatre Museum

Magna Plaza

St Nikolaaskerk

Detail of the Schreierstoren

Route 3

Stationsplein – Schreierstoren – Oude Kerk

This route starts at the station and covers the central part of the city to the east of the Damrak. It has to be said, however, that this is the part of the city, the old maritime quarter, which is now tainted by drug dealing and prostitution.

Bear left on the station concourse, pass the VVV Tourist Information Centre and look across the harbour basin above the mass of roofs and chimneys to the twin towers of the neo-baroque **St Nikolaaskerk**, which was built at the end of the 19th century.

Take the pedestrian subway under Prins Hendrikkade, but look out for No 85, **Batavia Huis**, where the facade is adorned with the terracotta heads of Indonesian women and elephants. The building once housed the offices of the Dutch East India Company; in 1619 the Dutch renamed Jakarta Batavia, and used it as a base from which to conquer Java and other Indonesian islands.

Before reaching the Geldersekade, a quick look down the pretty Oudezijds Kolk may cause some confusion. But yes, this is Amsterdam, not Venice! On the corner of the Geldersekade are the **Schreierstoren** ⓭, which were originally part of the city defences and directly adjacent to the harbour. The name for the towers is sometimes translated as the 'towers of tears', for it was here that wives and girlfriends often stood weeping as they waved farewell to their menfolk. The gable stone (1569) shows a sailing ship weighing anchor and a woman alone on the quayside.

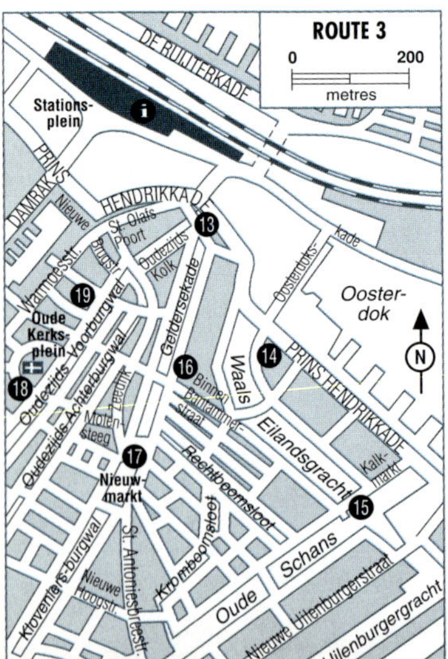

The ⋆ **Scheepvaart Huis** ⓮, on Prins Hendrikkade, has sometimes been likened to a ship, but it is in fact a classic example of the Amsterdam School of architecture that flourished early this century. It is covered inside and out with bas-reliefs of sea-horses, dolphins, seals, anchors, chains, etc. Four female forms on the cornices represent the four compass points while another embellishment over the entrance depicts the constellation of the Great Bear.

In the same street at No 131 lived Admiral de Ruyter, one of Holland's naval heroes who is buried in the Nieuwe Kerk (*see page 23*). The gable stone recalls the house's famous resident.

A little further along the Prins Hendrikkade is Kalkmarkt. It is well worth making a short detour to the **Nederlands Scheepvaart Museum** (Dutch Maritime Museum) in Kattenburgerplein (for opening times and details *see page 70*), where the glorious history of Holland as a seafaring nation is recorded. Another reminder of

Dutch maritime history is on view in De Werf 't Kromhout in Hoogte Kadijk. Formerly a shipyard, it is now a museum. At the turn of the century, 't Kromhout was one of Holland's biggest shipbuilding companies. The most impressive exhibit is a vessel from the East India Company fleet.

A continuation of Kalkmarkt is the Oude Schans and the **Montelbaanstoren** ⓯. This tower was constructed in 1512 as a fortification to defend the carpenters' workshops, a vital element in the prosperity of a town which depended on shipping and shipbuilding. The decorative Renaissance-style spire was added in 1606 by Hendrik de Keyser. This attractive fortified tower at a canal intersection is another favourite subject for amateur photographers. By the side of the Oude Schans at No 18, the name Jan Swammerdam (1637–80) is carved into the gable stone. Swammerdam, a zoologist, is widely recognised as the first scientist to identify red blood corpuscles.

On the east side of Oude Schans is the narrow street Recht Boomsloot running alongside a canal of the same name. This part of town has a higher proportion of warehouses, but they too display the characteristic gable ends with some fine examples of spout, neck and bell gables. The monumental flight of steps at No 22 is worth noting, as the original warehouse was converted into an Armenian Church in 1714.

Oriental restaurant

Running parallel to the north is **Binnen Bantammerstraat** ⓰, with its Chinese restaurants and casinos. These streets in Amsterdam's Chinatown are the subject of many bizarre rumours, and whether or not they are all well-founded, a large proportion of the local drugs trade is almost certainly masterminded from behind the tightly closed doors of this quarter. Yet despite the intrigue surrounding the area, the Oriental restaurants have earned an excellent reputation.

Binnen Bantammerstraat leads to Geldersekade and then Nieuwmarkt, an area which was badly disrupted by the underground construction work. These streets full of bars and clubs have now been renovated. Two of Hendrik de Keyser's houses in the Geldersekade (Nos 20 and 22) are protected by preservation orders.

Waag ⓱ (The Weigh-House) in Nieuwmarkt was originally a part of a turreted gate known as St Anthoniespoort. The gable stone is dated 1488, but the building's role as a maritime trading standards office did not begin until 1617, when the scales were installed. The upper floor served as the guildhall and each guild had its own entrance. One of the guildhalls, the stonemasons' guild (St Barbara) has been kept in its original state. The ornate interior décor is proof that the guild members were endowed with enormous skill.

The Waag

Jacob Hooy's Liquorice shop

In the Red Light District

The Oude Kerk

It is only a short walk from the weigh-house to Kloveniersburgwal. Jacob Hooy at No 12 have been in business for 200 years. As well as being Holland's leading supplier of all kinds of liquorice, the interior of the shop is almost a museum piece in itself. The bulbous sweet jars contain a vast selection of jet black titbits, sweet or salty, lavender or honey flavoured. Jacob Hooy also sell every kind of medicinal and culinary herb. Each one is stored in a small wooden drawer, the contents labelled with an enamel plate.

Return to Nieuwmarkt and cross the square diagonally to the Zeedijk. This is another street linked with Amsterdam's maritime history. Sailors' bars have given way to drug dealing and tourists are not advised to linger here, but to head north for only a few yards and then to turn into Molensteeg. This street marks the entry into Amsterdam's celebrated **red light district** or Walletjes.

Prostitutes even ply their trade in the Oudekerksplein in the shadow of Amsterdam's oldest church, the **Oude Kerk** ⓲. A wooden chapel once stood on this site, but in 1300 the foundations were laid for a triple-naved hall church. It was not finally completed until 1577. During some recent restoration work, the foundations of a central nave and two aisles were discovered, from which archaeologists have deduced that a transept was part of the original plans.

The stained glass in the north choir, showing scenes from the life of the Virgin, dates from 1555. The choir stalls, carved with lively scenes from the fables, the oak pulpit and the large organ are of special interest. The composer Jan P Sweelinck was once the organist here and music students from the Sweelinck Conservatory pay tribute to him by giving regular organ recitals. The programme of recitals is usually posted at the church entrance.

The church tower was finished in 1568, but one year later the Hemony brothers' carillon was added. There is a fine view over the roofs of the narrow gable houses from the top of the tower.

A Carillon Concert takes place here every Saturday from 4–5pm.

Continue the route northward along OZ Voorburgwal. At No 57 opposite the Oude Kerk is a distinctive step gable by Hendrik de Keyser. The facade's accolade arch is another interesting feature.

The merchant's house at No 40 OZ Voorburgwal, formerly a clandestine Catholic church, now houses the **Museum Amstelkring 'Ons' Lieve Heer op Zolder' ⓳** (Our Lord in the Attic). After the Reformation, when the public life of the city was presided over by Protestant authorities, Catholics were forced to conduct their worship in secret. Thus, the attic of this house, which was originally built for the merchant Jan Hartmann at the beginning of the 17th century, became a church. In the 18th century, it was enlarged by incorporating the storeroom of the adjoining house. The office for the clergy of St Nikolai remained here until 1887.

Until 1795, a period of around 200 years, this church was a place of worship for the Catholics of Amsterdam. Nowadays evidence has come to light that the authorities were well aware of the existence of this clandestine chapel, but decided not to persecute the worshippers for the sake of the well-being of the community.

In 1950, the whole building, now the property of a charity, was restored using public funds. The exhibits consist of the original church furniture, but also include paintings, silver and sacred objects from the secret church. It is also worth paying a visit to the adjoining house which has several rooms furnished in the original 17th- and 18th-century style.

The route back to the station leads through a maze of narrow lanes. Note the interesting facade and the step gable on De Leeuwenburg at the corner of OZ Armsteeg and OZ Voorburgwal.

On the corner of St Olofspoort and Nieuwe Burgsteeg is another fine example of a step gable. The house was at one time a bakery and the three men depicted on the gable stone are making *bollen*, a type of doughnut. It is only a few yards from here to Zeedijk 1, one of the oldest houses in Amsterdam. Note the horizontal weather-boarding on this house.

Take Nieuwe Brugsteeg and cross the bridge to reach the Damrak. The Stationsplein will be visible on the right.

Detail, Oude Kerk

Step gable, OZ Armsteeg

Bakers on gable stone

Route 4

Dam Square – Zuiderkerk – ★ Rembrandthuis – Synagogue – New Music Theatre – Rembrandtsplein

Outside Wijnand Fockinck

This route also begins at Dam Square. From the Hotel Krasnapolsky, turn into Pijlsteeg, where at No 31 is the **Wijnand Fockinck** ⓴, one of Amsterdam's best-known cafés and taster bars.

Here the friendly bar staff dispense the local spirits and liqueurs in tulip-shaped glasses. The glass will be so full that the customer needs to bend right over to take the first sip, otherwise there is a risk that, however steady the hand, some of the precious liquid will be spilt. The Wijnand Fockinck is not just another pub where drinkers stand for hours sinking one glass of spirits after another. It is an Amsterdam institution where Amsterdammers meet late in the afternoon, often on their way home from work, to while away the time before the evening meal.

The drinks here are genuine *jenever*, or liqueurs that were first distilled here in the 18th and 19th century, carrying quirky names such as 'Bride's Tears' or 'Parfait Amour'. The landlord is always happy to give his customers more information on what they have been drinking.

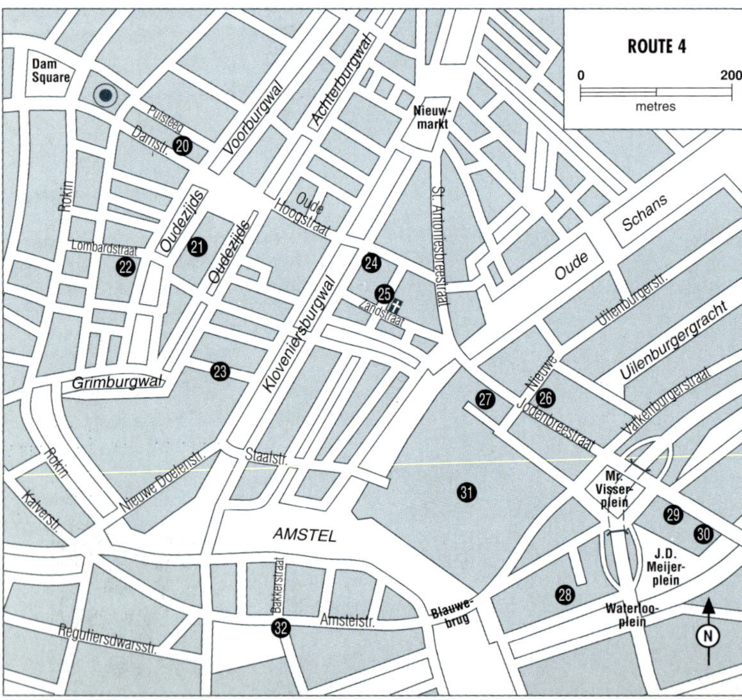

The Stadhuis is now a hotel

A copper coronet dangles from the ceiling and the tired shelves sag under the weight of bulky bottles.

Follow Pijlsteeg a little further, cross the bridge over OZ Voorburgwal, turn right and continue along the east bank to the old **Stadhuis** ㉑ (Town Hall). At one time a monastery stood on this spot but, after the Reformation, it was taken over by the Admiralty. When in 1808 Louis Bonaparte claimed what is now the Koninklijk Paleis as his official residence, the municipal authorities were forced out and moved in here. In 1927, the whole building was renovated and extended, so that all that remained of the original structure was the pillared facade, believed to be the work of Daniel Stalpaert. It is now a hotel.

The city council has now found new accommodation in the Stadhuis on Waterlooplein (*see page 36*). On the opposite bank of OZ Voorburgwal stands the old meat market, the municipal bank and pawnshop and the **Bank van Lening** ㉒. The oldest part of the building dates from 1550 and is actually in Lombardsteeg. It served as a peat store for the residents of nearby houses. The pawnshop was built in 1614 but the long facade which extended to the OZ Voorburgwal was not built until 1669. The entrance is the most remarkable feature and it bears all the hallmarks of master-builder Hendrik de Keyser.

Bank van Lening

OZ Voorburgwal ends at the Grimburgwal. Three canals meet at this point and the house which stands nearest to the junction is called **Huis op de Drie Grachten**. On the other side of the bridge is Gast Huys-Tor. The relief work above the entrance represents two sick men – an indication that the site used to be a hospital.

A passageway leads off Kloveniersburgwal to the left. This is **Oudemannhuispoort** ㉓ (Old Men's Home Gate). The gable stone depicts a pair of spectacles. A sign of old age perhaps? It is worthwhile browsing through the shelves of the second-hand and antiquarian bookshops.

Gable stone, Oudemannhuispoort

Oudemannhuispoort is also the entrance to the university courtyard with a statue of the goddess Athena.

Bust of Athena

Plaque to Hendrik de Keyser

Picturesque is certainly an adjective which can be attributed to **Kloveniersburgwal**. Follow this canal north to the junction with Oude Hoogstraat. On the opposite side of the canal at No 29 is the **Trippenhuis** ㉔, which was built by Justus Vingboons for the wealthy merchants Louis and Hendrik Trip. It is now the home of the Dutch Royal Academy of Science. The story is told that the narrow house at No 26 Kloveniersburgwal was built by the Trip brothers for a servant, who had apparently once said that he would be happy to live in a house that was no wider than the entrance (3m/9ft) to his master's house.

At the Kloveniersburgwal bridge, follow Nieuwe Hoogstraat to the **Zuiderkerk** ㉕ on Zandstraat. No longer used as a church, its main function now is as an exhibition centre, often for town planners to display plans for their next scheme. A permanent exhibition shows how the city has expanded, including information about recent renovation work in residential areas. It was built between 1603 and 1611 by Hendrik de Keyser as the first Protestant church after the Reformation. The chancel stands in the middle of this rectangular basilica-type, triple-nave church. Hendrik de Keyser is buried here, and so are three of Rembrandt's children.

Continue along Antoniesbreestraat, which then becomes Jodenbreestraat. Before World War II, this district was predominantly Jewish. Most of the inhabitants of the former **Jodenbuurt** ㉖ died in Nazi concentration camps. The badly damaged houses were demolished and the whole area bulldozed. The Joods Historisch Museum in the redundant synagogue on J D Meijerplein gives some idea of how this bustling area looked in its heyday.

The Rembrandthuis

Nos 4–6 Jodenbreestraat, opposite the textiles centre and university buildings, is the ★ **Rembrandthuis** ㉗. The world-famous painter Rembrandt Harmensz van Rijn (1606–69) became a wealthy and respected citizen of Amsterdam. He spent the most formative years of his life here in the heart of the Jewish quarter. Since 1906 the house has been in the care of a foundation which has been responsible for the restoration work and also for equipping the rooms with 17th-century furniture. The collection includes 250 etchings with a display that explains the technique. Other exhibits include some of his belongings and memorabilia (for opening times, *see page 70*).

Waterlooplein flea market

After so much exposure to the art world, take a relaxing walk to the **Waterlooplein** ㉘. Amsterdam's oldest and best-known flea market is located here. While the Muziektheater was under construction, the market was forced from its regular place, but it is now safely back on home ground.

A quick glance inside the **Portuguese-Israelite Synagogue** ㉙ will reveal the wealth of this small section of Amsterdam's Jewish community. The high barrel vault emphasises the size and the oak and Brazilian hardwood its riches. The huge copper candelabrum is lit every sabbath. Fully restored in the 1950s this synagogue is now regarded as the finest example of Jewish culture in the Netherlands.

Portuguese-Israelite Synagogue

The Dockworker Monument ㉚ on J D Meijerplein is the work of Mari Andriessen and it was erected to commemorate the Amsterdam dockworkers' uprising in February 1941. The workers protested vociferously against the deportation of their Jewish colleagues and fellow citizens, but the demonstrations were violently repressed by the German army of occupation. The Joods Historisch Museum is housed in the synagogue opposite.

The new concert hall and town hall, **Stadhuis** and **Muziektheater** ㉛, was opened in 1986. Austrian Wilhelm Holzbauer was responsible for the plans to build this huge structure. The main hall can accommodate 1,600 people and the stage extends over 22m (70ft). It is the home of the Dutch national ballet and opera companies as well as providing a venue for guest performances.

Cross the Amstel by the **Blauwbrug**. After the photogenic swing bridge, follow the bank of the Amstel to the right. This river, which gives the city its name, is formed from the confluence of the Drecht and the Kromme Mijdrecht in the lowlands to the southeast of the city. Turn left into the third narrow street, Backerstraat, to find **Rembrandtsplein** ㉜ with its many large cafés and bars and a monument to the great painter himself in the centre.

Statue of Rembrandt and café in Rembrandtsplein

Westerkerk nave and Rembrandt memorial plaque

Route 5

Jordaan – ** Anne Frank House

To the west of the Central Station, between Prinsen-, Brouwers-, Lijnbaans- and Looiersgracht is the district known as **Jordaan**. The word is said to be a corruption of the French word *jardin* meaning garden. There is evidence to show that in the 17th century this part of the town was mainly given over to vegetable growers who then sold their produce at the weekly market. Many of Amsterdam's folk songs make reference to Jordaan and, in particular, the Westerkerk tower, the Westertoren. Admittedly it is only on the edge of the district but the tower is visible from more or less everywhere. In the 1960s, this badly run-down quarter was discovered by the hippy community. Since then, the old houses, many with small, peaceful *hofjes* (*see page 66*) have been restored. A stroll around the narrow streets and alleys of Jordaan can be a relaxing experience.

The walk starts at the junction of the Prinsengracht and Radhuisstraat by the * **Westerkerk** (33). This Renaissance church was started in 1620, but was not completed until 1630 when Jacob van Campen added the tower. The tower is crowned with the blue, red and gold crown of Austria's Emperor Maximilian, a privilege bestowed on the people of Amsterdam when he was apparently cured of a fatal illness while in the town.

Designed by Hendrik de Keyser and finally consecrated in 1631, the 85-m (250-ft) tower is the tallest in the city and between the months of June and September it is open to the public. The chancel, the portal reliefs and the grating on the baptismal chapel all date from 1630. By the third column in the north wall is Rembrandt's tombstone, but it is a source of dispute among scholars as to whether his

A view of the Westerkerk Tower

remains do in fact lie inside. A marble memorial plaque was placed there in 1906. The great painter spent his last years in Jordaan at nearby Rozengracht 184 and he was buried in the Westerkerk in 1669. In 1966 the marriage of the then Crown Princess Beatrix to Claus von Amsberg took place here.

In 1944, in the merchant's house on the corner of Westermarkt and Prinsengracht a young Jewish girl from Frankfurt am Main, in hiding from the German occupying forces, wrote in her red diary: 'I believe in the basic goodness of humanity'.

Nowadays, that house, the ★★ **Anne Frank House** ㉞ on the Prinsengracht 263, has become an international place of pilgrimage (for opening times, *see page 68*). A staircase leads into the now famous backrooms where Otto Frank, his family and friends hid for two fraught years, from 1942 until August 1944. The house is a living monument to all the victims of Fascism and anti-Semitism. A small exhibition also documents the course of World War II as far as it affected the Jews of Amsterdam.

Statue of Anne Frank

Follow the Prinsengracht north as far as Prinsenstraat. At No 171 is **Zon's Hofje** ㉟. Originally this building was the simple community centre for the pacifist Protestant sect known as the Mennonites. Access to the *hofje* is via a long passage between two houses. The inner courtyard was added in the 18th century.

Returning to the Prinsengracht, at Nos 85–133 is the handsome **Hofje de Star** ㊱. The wealthy Christian merchant van Brienen had this almshouse built exclusively for the poor in his part of the community. The right-hand door next to the entrance is usually open. It leads to the warden's flat and the chapel. In the middle of the courtyard is an old pump with two pump handles. A notice informs users that drinking water is only available from one tap.

Leave the *hofje* and return along the Prinsengracht to Prinsenstraat. Cross the canal by the Prinsensluis bridge, then follow the left bank of the canal north to the **Noorderkerk** ㊲. It is assumed that the original design for this plain church was the work of Hendrik de Keyser. It was built between 1620 and 1623 by the city carpenter-in-chief Hendrik Staets and the ground plan of the church is in the shape of a Greek cross. Visitors wishing to view the church should contact the verger. On one of the outside

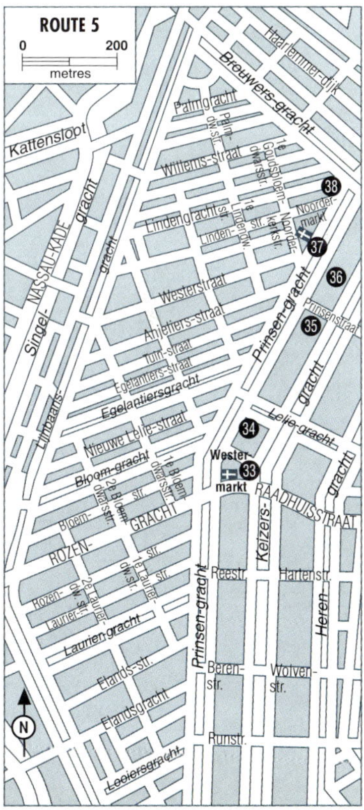

Papeneiland Café

The upside down world

King David gable stone

Doll shop in Karthuizerstraat

walls is a plaque to commemorate the demonstration held nearby on 24 February 1941 when hundreds of dock-workers protested against the deportation of their Jewish fellow citizens (*see page 37*).

On the Noordermarkt a pet and cage-bird market takes place every Saturday morning starting at 5am.

A series of handsome gables can be seen in the last section of the Prinsengracht as far as the Brouwersgracht. At the corner of the Prinsengracht and the Brouwersgracht it is well worth stopping for a coffee in **Papeneiland** ❸❽. With its old, glazed Delft tiles, the interior of this traditional Dutch café is fascinating, but the showpiece is without doubt the huge, cast-iron stove in a tiny room. Papeneiland marks the far northeast corner of the colourful Jordaan area (*see page 38*).

Behind Papeneiland Café turn into the Lindengracht. The facade at No 57 is of interest, as is the gable stone at No 53. The picture is described as the 'upside down world', in which fish fly around the tree tops and the name of the street is in mirror writing.

An interesting gable stone at Noorderkerkstraat No 14 depicts faith, love and hope.

A small detour through No 1E Goudsbloemstraat leads to the Palmgracht, where the Raepenhof (No 28) and the Bosschehofje (No 40) both date from 1648 and were built according to plans by Pieter A Raep.

At Lindengracht Nos 149–63 is the Suykerhof, which dates from 1667. Three gable stones in Lindenstraat, at Nos 4, 6 and 19 are carved with reliefs of King David.

The name Karthuizerstraat indicates that a Carthusian monastery once stood in this street. The four houses with the neck gables were built in 1737 and bear the names *Lente*, *Zomer*, *Herfst* and *Winter* (spring, summer, autumn and winter). The **Karthuizerhofje** was designed by master-builder Daniel Stalpaert in 1650. It served originally as a home for widows, but the small houses grouped around the grass with the two water pumps are now occupied by young people.

Karthuizerhofje

The De Zeven Keurvorsten *hofje* in Tuinstraat (Nos 197–223) has not yet been renovated. Despite their derelict appearance, the houses in the inner courtyard still display a certain elegance and it is worth taking a quick look.

On the corner of Eerste Egelantiersstraat and Dwarsstraat, the gable stone bears the inscription 'Claes Claeszhofje 1971' with a picture of the composer and organist Jan P Sweelinck playing a medieval instrument.

The lion fountain

A path from Dwarsstraat 3 leads to the **Claes Claesz and Anslo hofje**. The renovation and extension of this relatively large building took five years from 1968–73. Now many smart houses surround the four linked courtyards. In the last of the courtyards is a magnificent **lion fountain**. Leave the *hofje* by the path beside the Claes Claesz restaurant and turn right into Egelantierstraat. The houses at Nos 66–70 and 72–4 were restored with the assistance of the Diogenes Foundation. The aim of this organisation is to restore houses which are falling into disrepair, but it insists that the building then reverts to its original use.

Thanks to the row of splendid houses in the **Bloemgracht**, this street is sometimes known as Jordaan's Herengracht. The Dutch association for the protection of historic buildings, or the Hendrik de Keyser Society, owns Nos 87, 89 and 91 and Amsterdammers have subsequently christened these three houses the Drie Hendriken. The gable stones still bear the original names which were *seeman*, *landman* and *steeman*. Nos 83–5 has a perfect example of a twin neck gable. It is interesting to note how the windows become smaller. It is worth having a quick look at the many hundreds of beads in **Boutique 1001** on the other side of the canal (No 38).

Boutique 1001, the bead shop

The starting point for this walk, the Westerkerk, is easily reached from the eastern end of Bloemgracht. Those who wish to experience even more of Jordaan's charm can continue their tour into the southern part. Before turning right into Bloemstraat is de Eikeboom (oak tree), a fine example of a home and warehouse. Gable stone motifs often have symbolic significance. The anchor, for example, is an expression of hope. Find the bell-gabled house at Bloemstraat 5 for further examples. On the gable stone at Rosengracht 204–10, the inscription reads *In de swarte kasstoor*, a reference to the fact that at one time the house was used for the manufacture of hat felt from beavers' fur (*kasstoor*).

Inscribed gable stone

The Concertgebouw

Bust of Bach

Route 6

***Concertgebouw – **Stedelijk Museum – **Rijksmuseum Vincent van Gogh – ***Rijksmuseum – Vondelpark – Leidseplein**

To reach the starting point of this route, visitors are recommended to use public transport (*bus 26, 66, tram 3, 5, 12 or museum boat*).

On the corner of van Baerlestraat and de Lairessestraat is the ***Concertgebouw** ❸❾, built in 1887 by A L van Gendt. Since its completion, it has been home to the world-famous Concertgebouw orchestra (*see page 72*). A golden lyre stands on the roof above the entrance foyer and between the pillars on the projecting facade stand the busts of Beethoven, Sweelinck and Bach. In the course of its 100-year history, many famous composers and conductors have graced the podium. Names such as Brahms, Mahler, Richard Strauss, Stravinsky and Hindemith are a testimony to the esteem in which the orchestra is held.

Rehearsals, which are open to the public, take place every Wednesday around lunch-time, apart from during the summer break. Admission is free.

Opposite in Paulus Potterstraat are the new wing and sculpture garden of the ****Stedelijk Museum** ❹⓿ (Municipal Museum). The building which houses the museum was built in neo-Renaissance style at the end of the 19th century and the initial funds were bequeathed to the city by a wealthy widow. The collections include works by

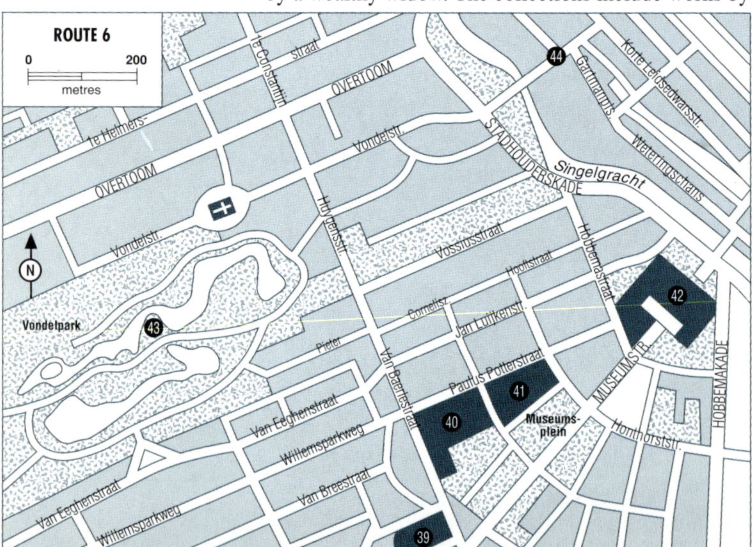

Dutch masters as well as by internationally renowned artists of the 19th and 20th century, such as van Gogh, Mondrian, Breitner, Israëls, Chagall, Kandinsky and Malevich. Next to the new wing is the sculpture garden, which contains numerous works by famous sculptors including Henry Moore (*Reclining Man*), Wouters (*Domestic Cares*), Wessel Couzijn (*Awakening of Africa*) and Volten (*Kubus*). (For opening times, *see page 71*).

The ★★ **Rijksmuseum Vincent van Gogh** ㊶ is next door to the Stedelijk Museum and houses 200 paintings and 500 drawings, as well as van Gogh's collection of Japanese wood carvings. There is also a library of letters including the full correspondence between the artist and his brother Theo. In addition, the gallery contains works by Toulouse-Lautrec, Gauguin, Monticelli and Bernard. (For opening times, *see page 71*).

Cheese carriers

Outside the Van Gogh Museum

Rijksmuseum

The first moves to make a collection of national works of art came in 1808 from the Dutch King Louis Bonaparte and culminated in 1885 with the opening of the ★★★ **Rijksmuseum** ㊷ (National Museum) (for opening times, *see page 71*), which was designed by P J H Cuypers. The first pieces of the collection were kept in rooms in the Koninklijk Paleis (*see page 22*) in Dam Square.

Rijksmuseum entrance

The new museum contains many loaned exhibits including dozens of portraits of regents and militia companies. Rembrandt's *The Night Watch* is the most outstanding example of this genre. There is also a full range of work by Dutch painters from the 15th century.

Both main entrances (the eastern entrance on the left and the western one on the right) are at Stadhouderskade 42. The entrance to the Department of Asiatic Art is at Hobbemastraat 19.

The main information desk is on the first floor landing. Reproductions and catalogues may be bought here. On the ground floor by the right-hand entrance is a restaurant, and the only place in the museum where smoking is permitted. Disabled visitors may use the lift and borrow a wheelchair.

Ground floor

Department of Dutch History (eastern entrance on the left), Rooms 101–14. This section contains paintings, ship models, arms, flags, religious objects, costumes, documents and memorabilia associated with Dutch political and military history. Many of the items belonged to former governors and the Admiralty, the East India and West Indies Company, and some come from private collections. The history of the 19th and 20th century is not covered in any great detail.

Model Ship Exhibit

Delftware and dolls' house

Department of Sculpture and Decorative Arts (western entrance on the right), Rooms 162–80. The exhibits here document the period from the Middle Ages to the beginning of the 20th century and on display are objects of ecclesiastical art, Dutch and French furniture, tapestries, silver, an apothecary's cabinet, as well as a collection of Delftware and dolls' houses.

18th- and 19th-century paintings (western entrance on the right), Rooms 142–9. The first few rooms mainly contain exhibits by painters from the Hague School, followed by works of the Amsterdam Impressionists.

Islamic Art (western entrance on the right), Rooms 138–41. The Islamic art section consists of carpets and ceramics from the 16th–18th centuries.

Copperplate engravings and library (entrance in Jan Luykenstraat 1), Rooms 128–33. These rooms display copperplate engravings by Dutch masters from the 15th–20th centuries, but there are also changing exhibitions of drawings and graphics from private collections.

First Floor

15th–17th century Dutch painting (main entrance), Rooms 201–36. Rooms 201 and 202 are devoted to the late Middle Ages with works by important painters such as Geertgen tot Sint Jans and Jan Mostaert.

Paintings representative of the Dutch Renaissance, which came almost a hundred years after the Italian Renaissance, are on display in rooms 203–9.

Dutch painting reached its zenith during the 17th century, Holland's Golden Age. The paintings of masters such as Frans Hals, Vermeer and Rembrandt hang in rooms

The Night Watch

210–28 along with the works of many other celebrated Dutch painters. On its own in room 224 is Rembrandt's masterpiece *The Night Watch*. The actual title is *The Company of Captain Frans Banning Cocq and Lieutenant Willem van Ruytenburch*.

Basement

Study collection (entrance in Jan Luykenstraat 1). The collection comprises some 800 paintings by Dutch masters.

Rembrandt: Self Portrait

Those with little interest in the Rijksmuseum should continue their tour from Paulus Potterstraat into P C Hooftstraat, one of the most exclusive shopping streets in Amsterdam. As well as antiques shops, there are expensive jewellers and *haute couture* fashion boutiques. The Konfiserie Godiva at No 68 is renowned for its pralines.

A good place for a stroll is the **Vondelpark** **43**. A sculpture entitled *The Virgin of Amsterdam* by A Linnemann stands at the entrance. The 45-hectare (120-acre) park was financed by wealthy Amsterdammers in the 19th century and is laid out on English lines with cycleways, footpaths and bridle tracks. Fishing is allowed in the streams and lakes. It is the biggest municipal park in Amsterdam, with a splendid rose garden and a little tea-house. The park is named after the Dutch poet Joost van Vondel, whose statue was unveiled here in 1867.

Delicacies for sale

For many years now, the park has been a favourite haunt for young people. Drug-users, buskers and young travellers were attracted here and the police became concerned about the rising incidence of muggings, so camping is no longer permitted within the park.

During the Middle Ages, the town gates stood on the **Leidseplein** **44**, which was also the mooring for boats which plied between Amsterdam and Leiden via the Haarlemmermeer. Now the most imposing feature is the magnificent art nouveau **American Hotel**, which has been a meeting place for artists and writers for years. A drink in the café downstairs is an ideal way to finish this tour.

American Hotel entrance

If the Rembrandtsplein is the centre of the cheaper end of Amsterdam's entertainment quarter, then the Leidseplein is the centre of the city's cultural life. Productions by the Amsterdam Theatre Group are usually performed in the Stadsschouwburg, a late 19th-century building. During the summer the cafés around the square are invariably full; in the winter too, the café owners are kept busy, as a part of the square is converted into an ice-skating rink.

Behind the Stadsschouwburg, de Melkweg (Lijnbaansgracht 243a), an old dairy, is now a very popular rendezvous for young people and in an old church in Weteringschans 6–8, the Paradiso has acquired quite a reputation as an alternative centre (*see page 91*).

Canal at Muiden

Muiderslot Castle

Castle detail

Excursion 1

Gooiland and the River Vecht – length of trip: approximately 100km (70miles)

This excursion takes in parts of the province of Noord-Holland as well as Utrecht. It starts in the Muiderberg, a sailor's paradise on IJsselmeer, and then continues through Gooiland. Here the landscape varies from cultivated fields to heathland interspersed with woodland. The small rivers and streams which meander through the undulating countryside are also typical of this region.

Leave the city in an easterly direction and follow the 231/A1 towards Amersfoort. The attraction of the small town of **Muiden** (pop. 7,000) is the moated castle of **Muiderslot**. It was built by Count Floris V to secure the mouth of the Vecht against the acquisitive bishops of Utrecht. After the death of the Count in 1296, the fortress was stormed by the same bishops. A new castle was built out of the ruins in 1370 and this remained the residence of the governors until 1795. Later the castle lost its influential status and became a prison. In the 17th century the chatelain, Pieter Cornelius Hooft, encouraged the foundation of the Muiderkring, a circle of artists and scholars which was to have considerable impact on the intellectual and cultural development of the area.

The popular recreation area of **Muiderberg** lies on the IJsselmeer only a few kilometres from the castle.

★**Naarden** (pop. 17,000), a small fortified town on the outskirts of Amsterdam, was founded in the 14th century after the destruction of an earlier settlement further north which bore the same name. In the 17th century the governor Willem III gave orders for the building of a new fortress. Following the guidelines of the Frenchman Vauban, the master builder of castles, Adriaan Dortsmann fortified the star-shaped ramparts with bastions and wide moats, which remain intact to this day.

At **Het Spaansehuis** (the Spanish House) in Turfpoortstraat, the picture on the corbel is a reminder of the bloodbath perpetrated in 1572, when the Spanish army murdered nearly all the inhabitants. Also worth seeing are the Stadhuis in the Netherlands Renaissance style and the painted wooden barrel vaulting of the Gothic Grote or St Vituskerk. The huge tower dominates the town and the surrounding countryside. The annual performance of the St Matthew Passion on Good Friday is world-famous.

The Spanish House

Radio Museum exhibit

Conceived as an artists' village, **Laren** (pop. 12,000) has lost nothing of its attraction for the visitor, even though the sheep are no longer driven to drink at the pond as they were at the turn of the century. At the **Singer Memorial Foundation**, the founder's private collection contains his own work and some influential sculpture and paintings from the 19th and 20th century.

Even such a spacious, modern, garden city such as **Hilversum** (pop. 95,000) has come to be regarded as a satellite of nearby Amsterdam. In this age of telecommunications, the name of the town has become synonymous with the Netherlands' most important television and radio transmission centre. The Omroepmuseum or **Radio Museum**, Melpad 34, displays a large collection of wireless equipment from the early days of radio technology up to the present.

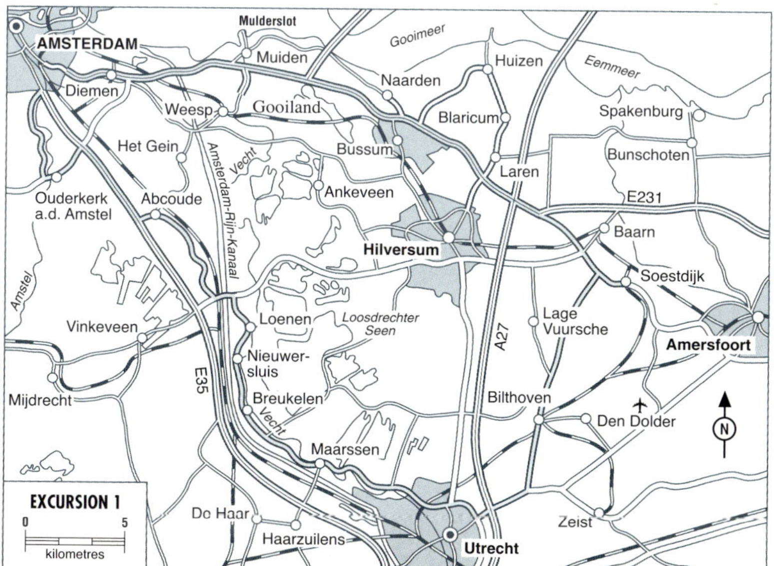

Hilversum Town Hall

Utrecht Cathedral tower

Statue outside the cloister

One of the most prominent sights in the town is the Gemeentehuis, the **Town Hall**, built according to plans by the famous architect W M Dudok between 1928 and 1930. Other examples of his work in the town centre are the Cubist-style public buildings.

On Schuttersweg, there is an historic apiary, which is open to the public from 1 April to the end of September (tel: 0 35 4 12 84).

The journey continues through wooded Gooiland towards Soestdijk. It is well worth making the 3-km (2-mile) detour to **Lage Vuursche** and the castle of Drakestein. Built in 1640 and completely restored in 1963, it was the home of the former Crown Princess Beatrix and Prince Claus. The octagonal house with its large annexe is surrounded by a moat and stands in a pleasant English-style park. It is not open to visitors. Queen Juliana and Prince Bernhard, the parents of the queen, live in the white castle of **Soestdijk**, which was originally built as a hunting palace. A panoramic view of the castle can be obtained from the road.

At the junction with the road to Bilthoven stands a statue to the Prussian sentry Christoffel Pullmann, who lost his life defending the then Prince Willem from an attack by revolutionaries.

Those not wishing to include Utrecht in the day's programme can skirt around the north of the city on the ring road. A romantic boat trip past elegant 19th-century villas on the gently flowing River Vecht makes a splendid alternative.

Detour to Utrecht and Doorn

★ **Utrecht** (pop. 439,000) was once a Roman fortress, then a Frankish castle and finally the bishops' seat and cultural centre of the province of the same name. Impressive monasteries, grandiose Renaissance and delicate rococo portals and, most importantly, the churches, which are of particular interest to art historians, have been carefully preserved as evidence of the city's glittering past.

The cathedral on the Domplein must be seen first. It was built in the 13th and 14th centuries on the site of a Roman castle and a 10th-century minster church. All that remains standing are the transept and tower, the tallest church tower in the Netherlands at 113m (370ft). The nave collapsed in a storm in 1674 and was never rebuilt. The chapter room, which is joined to the church by a Gothic cloister, is now the main assembly hall of the university.

Traces of a building dating from even earlier times were also uncovered at the site of the 13th-century early Gothic Geertekerk. This building was destroyed by iconoclasts in 1566. The history of the Jakobikerk also goes back even further, to the 12th century. During the late Middle Ages pilgrims came here en route to the grave of St James in Santiago de Compostela in Spain. The church was rebuilt many times and admirably restored in 1969.

Situated on a backwater of the Rhine, the town contains much more evidence of having been a prosperous merchant settlement. Beautiful patrician houses line the Kromme Nieuwe Gracht, and in Lange Niewstraat stand the Vleeshal (meat market), built in 1432, and the 16th-century convent church of St Catherine. Dating from 1636, the Maliebaan is one of the finest promenades in the Netherlands.

Information: VVV Tourist Information Centre, Vredenburg 90, NL 3511 BD Utrecht.

In the museum at St Catherine's convent

The castle of **Doorn** (town pop. 11,000), just 12km (8 miles) southeast of Utrecht, was once the seat of the noble Ridderhofstad. It was built by the Bishop of Utrecht in the 14th century to protect the surrounding territory. From 1920 to 1941 the last German kaiser, Wilhelm III, spent his last years in exile there and is buried in the mausoleum.

In the castle at nearby **Zeist** (pop. 60,000) memorabilia of the Moravian brotherhood can be seen.

To the west of Utrecht lies **Haarzuilens**. The rather tasteless picture book castle, De Haar, was erected at the end of the 19th century in the style of a medieval fortress. The building, with its surrounding courtyard, is still the private property of Baron van Zuylen. It is worth having a look at the interior for the opulent decoration.

On the return journey to Amsterdam, about 7km (4 miles) from Haarzuilens, is **Breukelen** (pop. 10,000). In the parish church there is a memorial tablet to the Pilgrim

De Haar Castle, Haarzuilens

Doorn Castle

Aspects of Nyenrode Castle

Fathers, who named the New York district of Brooklyn after this pretty village. The numerous castles and country seats nearby are not open to the public. Those of particular interest include Gunterstein, a 13th–14th-century knight's castle; 13th-century **Nyenrode** with a carillon in the tower and the 18th-century Queekhooven with a beautifully laid out garden. Just north of Breukelen the road passes the Vreedenhoff estate in Nieuwersluis.

Loenen, just to the north, has managed to preserve the essential character of the old Netherlands. The white bascule bridge over the Vecht is a prominent landmark.

The area around **Abcoude**, a pretty town at the confluence of three rivers, is splendid walking country.

The **Loosdrechter lakes** lie to the east of Loenen. Boat trips leave from Oud-Loosdrecht, Oud-Loosdrechtsedijk 165–7 at hourly intervals from April to the middle of October. Regattas are also held here.

Ouderkerk aan de Amstel. This picturesque spot can only be described as the archetypal Dutch village. In summer, visitors can enjoy a drink at a delightful inn in the middle of the village, on the green banks of the Amstel. The Portuguese-Israelite cemetery, founded in 1614, with its weathered gravestones bearing Portuguese and Hebrew inscriptions, is of interest and the Levi de Barrios, the married couple portrayed in Rembrandt's painting *The Jewish Bride*, are buried here.

The Amstel leads back to Amsterdam. On the outskirts of the town on the left-hand side stands a **statue of Rembrandt**, sketchbook in hand. He is one of several 17th-century Dutch artists who are understood to have found inspiration in the landscapes of this area.

Rembrandt statue

Excursion 2

Around the old Haarlemmermeer – length of trip: approximately 75km (45 miles)

This excursion takes the visitor to the southeast of Amsterdam. Unfortunately it is impossible to by-pass the towns of Buitenveldert and Amstelveen on the outskirts of Amsterdam before reaching **Schiphol** 10km (7 miles) away. The name of the airport derives from *scheepsel*, which means 'ships' hell', a reminder of the terrible storm, which led to the reclamation of the Haarlemmermeer after it was drained in 1852.

In 1917 a small military airfield was built which eventually developed into one of the world's great international airports. The best overall view of the site is obtained from the large roof terrace. One of the unusual features of this airport is that the runways are 4m (12ft) below sea level. A visit to the **Aviodome**, the museum of flight technology, can be very rewarding. Historic models, modern engines and electronic equipment are displayed beneath the roof of the striking dome-shaped building.

Aviodome exhibit

Aalsmeer (pop. 22,000), once a tiny fishing village southwest of Amsterdam, now lies on the Ring Canal of the Haarlemmermeer *polder* and is reputed to be the biggest flower market in the world. In 1830 when the Haarlemmermeer threatened to overwhelm the university town of Leiden after three larger villages had already been devastated by the flood tides, a commission was set up in The Hague to devise ways of overcoming such natural disasters. Soon afterwards a plan was drawn up, utilising all the available technology. As a result, the 'sea-wolf', the local term for the stormy sea, was tamed. The draining of the area was achieved by two great steam engines, one of which can still be seen at Vijfhuizen near Heemstede. The fertile soil of the reclaimed land now supports fifteen thriving villages and hamlets. Most of them can be seen on this route.

Aalsmeer

Even in the Middle Ages, the inhabitants of the seaside village of Aalsmeer grew lilacs, strawberries and winter cabbage and sold their produce in the markets in Amsterdam. Now the farmers supply the nearby city with all its fresh vegetables. As well as the cultivation of vegetables, large areas of this flat land have been given over to the cultivation of roses. Every year 500 million of these beautiful flowers are exported all over the world. Visits can be made to the Centrale Aalsmeerse Veiling, Legmeerdijk 313, Monday to Friday 7.45–11am. Auctions of cut flowers and pot plants also take place here.

Aalsmeer flower auction

The Mennonites have lived in Aalsmeer since they fled the persecution of the Spaniards in the 16th century. Much of this area was then impenetrable peat bog. Many still live on tiny islands by the Uiterweg, the road which leads to the Westeinder lake. The islands are now connected to the main road by narrow footbridges and swing bridges.

For more information, contact VVV Tourist Information Centre, Stationsweg 8.

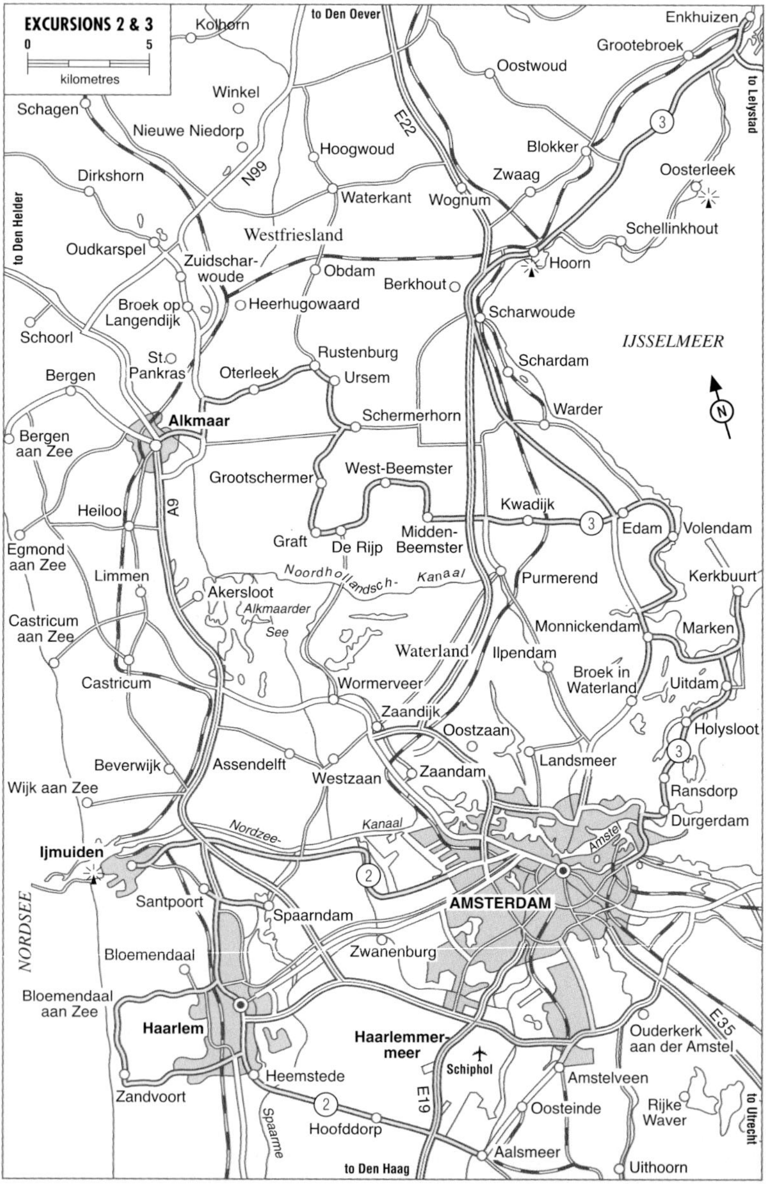

Those travelling by car should continue along the Haarlemmermeerpolder towards Heemstede, a suburb of Haarlem. Shortly before the signpost a road turns off to the right leading to the **Cruquius Poldermuseum**, which is visible from the road. This museum contains displays and information on the draining of the *polders*.

★★ **Keukenhof** hosts the greatest open-air flower show in the world and attracts hundreds of thousands of visitors each year with its display of 6–7 million tulips, narcissus and hyacinths.

Zandvoort (pop. 15,000). This is an internationally-renowned resort with a casino and a 4.2-km (2-mile) long motor-racing track and offers a blend of traditional and modern comforts. The nearby resort of Bloemendaal aan Zee has also retained some of its turn of the century charm.

★ **Haarlem** (pop. 160,000) is the capital of the province of Noord-Holland and along with Delft and Leiden possesses an old town, which is still largely intact. At the centre of the town is the ★ **Grote Markt**. Originally this was the tournament square of the Dutch counts, but over the years, civic buildings have come to dominate the square.

The lead-faced wooden tower of the Late Gothic ★★ **St Bavokerk** or **Grote Kerk** is 80m (250 ft) high. The church was erected over the grave of St Bavo and the famous Dutch painter Frans Hals is also buried here. Opposite the church, on the spot where the Count Palatine rose in rebellion, stands the Raadhuis (town hall). Next to the Grote Kerk the ornate Renaissance facade of the Vleeshal (meat market and guildhall) is particularly striking. Of great interest is the ★★ **Frans Hals Museum** in Groot Heiligland, displaying many portraits by the Dutch artist.

IJmuiden is the port at the mouth of the Noordzee Kanal, which was dug in 1876 to connect Amsterdam with the open sea. Saturday morning is the best time to see the passing ships and the best view is from the road which runs over the enormous lock complex. A walk along the harbour moles is occasionally possible.

The fish dock, the biggest in the Netherlands, and the fish auction (Monday to Friday 7–11am) are among the main attractions of this busy port. Local companies organise deep-sea fishing trips for anglers from here.

For more information, contact: VVV Tourist Information Centre, Marktplein 42.

Spaarndam is a typical dyke village with a windmill and five locks. It was here that a small boy by the name of Hans Brinker is said to have saved his village from flooding by stopping a tiny leak in the dyke with his finger. His statue stands in the centre of the village.

A short walk leads to neighbouring **Spaarnwoude** with its unusual village church. About 21km (12 miles) from Amsterdam, it is an attractive and relaxing spot.

Flower show poster

IJmuiden port

Hans Brinker

Excursion 3

Zuider Zee, Westfriesland, Zaanland – length of trip: approximately 106km (70 miles)

This excursion (*see Map, page 52*) crosses the IJ into Waterland, skirts the low-lying areas in the province of Noord-Holland, southern West Friesland and finishes in Zaanland. The detour to Hoorn and Enkhuizen could be taken as a separate excursion.

When leaving Amsterdam follow the signs to Amsterdam Noord, crossing the IJ by the Schellingwouderbrug. From this new bridge, there is a superb view across the eastern outskirts of the city with the IJ on the left and the Buiten-IJ on the right. At the first junction on the north bank take a right turning in the direction of Durgerdam. This stretch of road runs along the foot of the old Zuider Zee dyke.

Durgerdam

Durgerdam is an attractive settlement with a row of pointed wooden gables in the centre of the village. The building with the cupola was originally the town hall. Continue along the Waterland See dyke to Kinselmeer. Between Durgerdam and Kinselmeer is a turning to Ransdorp, whose tower dominates the flat landscape. Isolated Holysloot with its narrow bridges and tiny houses is one of the most charming villages in the Waterland district and can only be reached via Ransdorp.

Harbour in Marken

The route along the dykes to Uitdam passes through some charming countryside, as does the short walk from Uitdammer Diep to Holysloot. But those in a hurry should follow signs to **Marken**, formerly an island in the IJsselmeer which was cut off from the mainland by a high tide in 1164. Before the bay was closed off by a barrage dam in 1932, Marken was often left almost completely submerged by the autumn and winter gales. Of the original ten hamlets only seven still remain and the houses, which until 1931 were built exclusively of wood, still stand on tarred stilts, making an interesting photograph for the many tourists. Many of the conservative Calvinist population still wear 18th-century costume. Their colourful garments are of the kind worn when the men went whaling in the Arctic Sea and the women stayed behind to look after the smallholdings. But after the dyking of the Zuider Zee fishing no longer gave them a livelihood and tourism has increasingly taken its place.

Traditional costume

The scene on a market day in the summer can seem like a step back in time. Picturesque **Kerkbuurt**, the main village, is quite remarkable. The women's costumes consist of multi-coloured skirts, bodices and square bonnets. Young boys and girls are also dressed in traditional costumes, their hair in magnificent curls set with sugar water.

And then there are the green-painted cottages, their tiny rooms decorated with colourful shelves, caskets, cornices, cupboards and box-beds, all reminiscent of a dolls' house. One of the houses, Sijtje Boes, may be visited.

Return to the mainland and follow signs to **Monnickendam** (9km/6 miles), at the heart of the Waterland and one of the oldest towns in Holland. The medieval harbour was constructed in the 15th century. Particularly decorative are the weigh-house built in 1660, the 1591 bell tower and the north porch of the Nikolaikerk which dates from the middle of the 16th century. The marriage hall in the 18th-century town hall may be visited. Beside the harbour is the Stuttenburg Restaurant, which not only serves very good fish but also houses an interesting collection of old mechanical musical instruments which are sometimes played to entertain customers.

In the summer, a small ferry plies across the Gouwzee between Marken and Monnickendam.

Volendam (pop. 24,000) is regarded by many as the quintessential small Dutch town. The local people still wear traditional costumes, and not just for tourists but as part of everyday life. The women's pretty, hand-made lace bonnets may be bought as souvenirs, as may coral necklaces and woollen scarves, sold in the many tourist shops along the harbour. The special costumes are worn mainly for festivals and for church on Sunday. During the week, the older women exchange the lace bonnet for a pointed cap of coarse black cotton. Sometimes old fishermen can be seen wearing red pantaloons.

Some of the old stilt houses can still be seen in the nearby hamlet of **Slobbeland**, and the picturesque fishing

Cottage interior, Kerkbuurt

Volendam

Volendam on the Zuider Zee

harbour must certainly be included in any sightseeing programme. Monday is still washing day here and it is not uncommon to see clothes hanging out in the street.

There is an interesting collection of old paintings in the Spaander Hotel situated beside the harbour. Costumes and models of fishing vessels are displayed in the Folk Museum at Klosterbuurt 5.

Cheese shop in Edam

★★ **Edam** (pop. 24,000). Even though the town had its heyday between the 16th and 18th centuries, herring fishing and cheese still contribute to its prosperity. This old town on the southwestern banks of the IJsselmeer lies at the heart of the Markerwaard *polder* country and the following circular walk includes all the main sights. Start from the car park on the Scheepsmakersdijk (the shipbuilders' dyke): on the right stands the house of the Dyke Builders' Association with its pretty front garden. On the opposite bank are two 18th-century tea pavilions. Cross Doelenstraat, with the Kwakel bridge on the left and the bell tower in the background, and continue to Doelland with the town's last small shipyard on the left. Turn left over the bridge and through Spuistraat to the corner of Keizersgracht. Then turn right into the Damplein, a square built in the form of an arched bridge, where it is worth having a look at the 1737 Stadhuis with its wooden tower, the Registry Office, where the floor is still strewn with sand as in the Middle Ages, and the **Stedelijk Museum**. The floating cellar of this museum is shaped liked the stern of a ship. Among the curiosities of the Town Museum are the portraits of three extraordinary Edam citizens: the 2.6-m (8-ft) tall Trijnte Kever, the 200-kilo (455-lb) heavyweight Jan Claesz and the mayor Pieter Dirksz Langebaard who, with his 2.5-m (8-ft) long beard, collected money at fairs for the orphans of Edam.

Pieter Dirksz Langebaard

Continue the walk across the Kai des Voorhaven to the double bascule bridge. The opposite side leads back to the dam. Follow Breestraat as far as the Achterhaven where there is a wooden Gothic house dating from 1500. At the end of Batenburgerstraat turn right into Kerkstraat. No 23 is the site of an old orphanage and Nos 30 and 32 have particularly attractive gables. Turn left through the Grote Molensteeg to the small Nieuwe Vaartje canal and continue in the direction of the old moat. Pass the church and churchyard on the left and then cross the Matthijs-Tinxgracht quay to the **Kaasmarkt** (cheese market) with its 16th-century weigh-house. Continue along Prinsenstraat, turn right before the bridge and along Kleine Kerkstraat to the bell tower (formerly the Church of Our Lady). Cross the Lingerzijde and the bridge to return to the starting point, a distance of around 3.5km (2 miles).

Detail, old orphanage

Information: VVV Tourist Information Centre, (Speeltoren) Damplein 1, NL-1135 BK Edam.

Detour to Hoorn and Enkhuizen

★★ **Hoorn** (pop. 55,000), situated on the wide bay of the Markerwaard, was once the capital of Westfriesland and a flourishing trading centre. Food production and metal and wood processing are the main industries of this bustling town, whose courageous seafarers gave their name to Cape Horn at the southern tip of South America. The town has a number of excellent, well-maintained buildings and the major sights include the 1532 Hoofdtoren (harbour tower), with its quay and warehouses; the Waage (weigh-house) on Rode Steen, built in 1609 according to Hendrik de Keyser's plans; the West Friesland Museum in the Proostenhuis, originally the assembly building for the Council of Westfriesland; the 15th-century Noorderkerk with its Renaissance choir stalls; warehouses which belonged to the East India Company on Munstraat and the 1613 Town Hall in Nieuwstraat, where the council chamber was built in Louis XVI style.

Information: VVV Tourist Information Office, Rode Steen 2, NL-1621 CV Hoorn.

A wet day in Hoorn

Enkhuizen

★★ **Enkhuizen** (pop. 16,000). This town on the west bank of the IJsselmeer is criss-crossed by a network of small canals. It has a fine historic centre and is surrounded in spring by vast fields of flowers. Today the people of this once flourishing port earn their living from fishing, tourism and the sale of seeds. Enkhuizen has many churches, but perhaps the 15th-century Gothic **Westerkerk** has most to offer. Its treasures include a carved wooden choir-screen and a 17th-century library. The gabled red-brick houses with their forward-leaning facades are an unusual sight and experts still disagree as to whether they were deliberately built 'out of alignment' (*see page 65*), or whether it is simply old age which has caused them to lean. In the outdoor **Zuider Zee Museum**, only reached by boat from

Wierdijk 18, houses have been transported from other parts of the region and rebuilt. The reconstructed village gives an insight into life around the former Zuider Zee. Weddings are still held in the village church.

From June to the middle of August small pleasure boats cross to the fishing village of Urk in Noordoostpolder on the opposite side of the Markerwaard. In April and May, a cycle tour through the bulb fields around Enkhuizen is the ideal way to see this corner of Holland. The 30-km (20-mile) *damm* or embankment road across the IJsselmeer to Lelystad, which separates the IJsselmeer from the Markerwaard, begins just south of Enkhuizen.

Details: Beemster…
and De Rijp town halls

Continue the round trip in a westerly direction towards the polderland of **Beemster** via Kwadijk, Midden-Beemster, De Rijp, Graft, Schermerhoorn, Ursem, Oterleek to Alkmaar (approximately 35 km/22 miles).

Around 1612 this polderland was drained by twenty-six windmills. The plans of Jan Adriaanszoon Leeghwater, who was a specialist in marshland drainage, were used for the work. The old farmhouses protected by saddle roofs and the many well-maintained windmills are typical of this wide pastoral landscape.

This stretch of countryside between Edam and Oterleek and almost to the outskirts of Alkmaar, must be one of the most beautiful in the whole of the Netherlands. Small museums such as the House of the Pastor's Wife, Betje Wolff, at Midden-Beemster (Middenweg 178) and the Folk Museum in the Houten Huis at De Rijp (Rechtestraat 146) provide background information on local history.

Cheese carriers

Alkmaar (pop. 88,000) is best visited between the end of April and the end of September and, if possible, on Friday mornings between 10am and noon, when the world-famous cheese market is held. Taking the **Kaasmarkt** express from Amsterdam Central Station can save time.

Traditionally the cheese carriers are dressed entirely in white and wear straw hats in one of the four guild colours. At a running pace they carry sometimes as many as 80 medium-sized cheeses on a gondola-shaped carrier from the warehouses to the weigh-house and then to the lorry waiting in the background. Cheese tasting is another part of the lavish show laid on for tourists. But the real business takes place within the walls of the exchange.

Grote Kerk

Among the many sights in the town is the **Grote Kerk**. Built in the Brabant Late Gothic style with a cruciform basilica, it has striking, painted vaulting and the oldest organ in the Netherlands. This Renaissance organ is played on market days between 11am and 12.15pm. Of interest to art historians is the Late Gothic east wing of the Stadhuis at Langestraat 97. The west wing was added in 1694 and the facade altered in the 19th century. The Polder Room and the Magistrates' Conference Room may be visited.

The Waag or weigh-house on Waagplein was originally a medieval naved chapel and in the restored **Cheese Museum**, also on Waagplein, visitors can learn more about cheese making. A stroll through the Hofje van Spilinter (Ritzevoort 2) is a relaxing way to end this short walk through the town.

There are two trips worth taking from Alkmaar. To the north is Broek op Langedijk or Zuidscharwoude, in the Land of the Thousand Islands, as it is called, where cabbage is grown on a large scale. A visit to the vegetable auction in Broeker Veiling can also be quite an experience. The boats laden with produce go straight to the auction hall. Bergen and Bergen aan Zee are famous for their unusual sand dunes.

The journey from Alkmaar back to Amsterdam passes through Alkersloot on the Alkmaardermeer. Before reaching Wormerveer, the road goes through the middle of Zaanland, the oldest industrial district of the Netherlands, before it reaches the *polder* country around Zaandijk.

★ **Zaanse Schans.** This open-air museum outside Zaandam offers the perfect, stereotypical picture book image of Holland. The aim of the museum foundation is to buy old wooden houses and windmills threatened with demolition and to rebuild them on this site.

And finally to **Zaandam** where the statue of Peter the Great on the dam is a memorial to the time when he is said to have lived incognito in a timber cottage, the Czaar Peterhuisje at Krimp 24, and learnt the carpenter's trade. The truth has never been established, but the legend achieved immortality through an opera by G A Lortzing, entitled *The Czar and the Carpenter.*

On the beach at Bergen aan Zee

Open-air museum, Zaanse Schans

TOT EN MET 26 SEPTEMBER
SHOWPIECES FROM THE GOLDEN AGE

Art History

Opposite: Nieuwe Kerk

The Amsterdam of the 16th century was enclosed by the Geldersekade, the Kloveniersburgwal and the Singel. To the east, by the present-day Oude Schans, were the municipal shipwrights.

There are few buildings of historic interest which predate the beginning of the 17th century, Amsterdam's Golden Age. The Oude Kerk (Old Church) and the Late Gothic Nieuwe Kerk are obvious exceptions. The Schreierstoren, St Anthony's Gate (the Waag), the Munttoren, plus one dwelling in the Begijnhof 34 and Zeedijk 1 have been partly preserved. All of these date from the first phase of the city's development.

Oude Kerk interior

The marshy subsoil posed much the same problems for architects then as it does today, but while the builders of the past were obliged to build their houses without basements and used hundreds of piers in the marshy soil, new techniques and materials have permitted architecture of gigantic proportions, even in the heart of the city. The latest example is the new opera house or Stopera on the Waterlooplein.

The Golden Age (17th century)

At the end of the 16th century, the town was enlarged by one ring as far as the Herengracht and Rapenburgerstraat. In 1612, the Three Canal Plan of Hendrik Staets was implemented. It was his idea to develop the town in the now familiar pattern of concentric rings. But it was at this time that the name of Hendrik de Keyser (1565–1621) came to the fore. First the Zuiderkerk and then the old stock exchange were built according to his plans. The latter, which has now been demolished, was in the same style as the London Stock Exchange. He was later responsible for embellishing the towers of the Montelbaan and the Mint Tower (Munttoren) in Renaissance style. He designed the patrician houses on the canal banks and began work on the Westerkerk, the most popular church in the city. It too is built in Renaissance style but much of the work was completed after his death by his son Pieter. The Rembrandthuis in Jodenbreestraat 4–6 also dates from this period. The association for the protection of historic buildings is called the Hendrik de Keyser Society.

Westerkerk

After Keyser, it was the master builder Jacob van Campen (1595–1657) who left an impressive legacy to the city. He built houses by the canals for many of the wealthy merchants (Keizersgracht 177), worked on castles for the House of Orange and developed plans for the first theatre (1637). He achieved lasting fame, however, for his contribution to Amsterdam's town hall (Koninklijk Paleis), which was completed by Daniel Stalpaert. Jacob van

Koninklijk Palace, interior

Canal-side facades

House in Herengracht

Campen is also believed to have been responsible for the pilaster facade on the pretty town orphanage in Kalverstraat. He was Holland's master of the classical style.

The man who is associated most closely with the canal-side facades is Philip Vingboons. Some examples of his work can be seen at the Herengracht 168, 364–70, 412, 450 and the Keizersgracht 319. His son Justus Vingboons designed the plans for the impressive staircase at the Royal Academy of Science at Kloveniersburgwal 29.

One distinctive feature of the facades from that period is the sense of harmony and balance that the architects achieved, but at the same time each house has its own unique style. It should be remembered, however, that this consistency was only achieved because of the strict building regulations which were imposed at the time.

Frans Hals (1580–1666) is regarded as the founder of the Dutch school of realistic painting. Often called 'the first modern painter', he introduced to fine art the emotion of the moment, a glance or grimmace that might be seen anywhere on the streets, but nowhere in the posed, stilted portraiture of the past. His work was commissioned by the wealthy citizens of Amsterdam, by patricians and scholars including the French philosopher Descartes. His lively, flowing paintings such as *The Laughing Cavalier* (in London) and *The Merry Drinker* (Rijksmuseum) are world-famous. His spirited brushwork is reminiscent of the Impressionists, but his portraits always reflected the dignified demeanour of his subjects.

De Staalmeesters by Rembrandt

Few, however, would doubt that the Golden Age painter with the greatest reputation, then as now, was Rembrandt Harmensz van Rijn (1606–69), who started painting in his native Leiden but spent his most productive years living and working in Amsterdam. His work comprised 600 paintings, 300 etchings and 1,500 drawings. His skilful use of light and shadow is a source of wonder for modern painters. It accentuated the intensity of the scenes he portrayed and focused attention on the emotional tension of the subject.

Like other leading members of the Dutch School, Rembrandt broke new ground in realism. One of his most daring, and most costly, paintings was his 1642 masterpiece *The Night Watch*, a study of members of a local militia band. The large painting now has pride of place in the Rijksmuseum, but was apparently not well received at the time because it was regarded as too casual and haphazard. This condemned Rembrandt to a period of unpopularity, leading to bankruptcy; fewer commissions meant that he could no longer support his extravagant lifestyle. Rembrandt died a pauper.

Vermeer: Head of a Girl

Jan Vermeer (1632–75) worked in Delft and produced only about 40 paintings in his life, but he, too, is regarded as one of the great masters of Dutch painting.

The 17th century did not just produce great architects and painters. A Quellinus the Elder is regarded as Holland's greatest sculptor. Jacob van Campen brought him to Amsterdam and gave him the task of completing the stone-carving work for the Royal Palace (*see page 22*).

Rombout Verhulst (1624–98) worked with van Campen and de Keyser on the tombstones of many famous admirals (*see Nieuwe Kerk, page 61*) and also on a number of memorials in the city centre.

Furniture, Our Lord in the Attic; porcelain in the Rijksmuseum

The most famous poets of the 17th century were Joost van den Vondel and Pieter Cornelis.

The city's printers, free from the restraints of censorship, published first editions which were frequently controversial in both political and religious circles. Dutch cartographers have always been highly regarded, as has the work of the city's artisans. Furniture, glass, faience pottery (Bont), Amstel porcelain and tapestries were in demand all over the world.

The scholars of that time were engaged in lively debate on spiritual and philosophical matters and their discussions owed much to the Portuguese Sephardic and German Jewish backgrounds of the leading figures. Although born in Amsterdam of Portuguese parents in 1632, Spinoza was one such influential philosopher, who was eventually ostracised by the Jewish community for his views. Not only did many scholars and artists come from Jewish backgrounds, but many of the patrons of the arts who encouraged creativity also had Jewish origins.

Amsterdam became Holland's literary centre, with circles of aesthetes *(Muiderkring)*, groups of poets *(Nil Volentibus Arduum)*, famous magazines *(De Gids)* and influential publishers.

Centraal Station with exterior detail

18th and 19th century

It was becoming hard to find evidence of Dutch artistic merit at the end of the 17th century. In the 18th century, French classicism was informing nearly all artistic expression. In Holland as in the rest of Europe, architectural style in the 19th century copied earlier styles and examples can be seen at the Centraal Station and the Rijksmuseum (*see page 43*). Both were designed by P J H Cuypers. Vincent van Gogh, is of course, the best-known 19th-century Dutch painter.

20th century

Most modern Dutch architects have wanted to look forward rather than back. H P Berlage (1856–1934) made one of the most interesting contributions to Expressionism. His Koopmansbeurs (Stock Exchange), built in 1899–1903, is of particular interest (*see page 20*). Evidence of this New Realism can also be found in much of his residential architecture.

The painters Piet Mondrian (1872–1944) and Kees van Dongen (1877–1968) have earned prominent places in the history of modern art. Mondrian's work benefited from his encounters with Matisse and the French cubist movement. Dongen started producing neo-Impressionist landscapes, but at the beginning of the 20th century he came under the influence of the Fauves. In 1917, the painter Theo van Doesburg founded the magazine *De Stijl*, enabling painters, architects and writers to give expression to their views on art and society. Mondrian also expounded his theories in the magazine.

In the post-war period, a band of Dutch, Belgian and Danish painters including Appel, Corneille and Constant founded the Cobra group and published a magazine with the same name.

Houses and Courtyards

Canal-side houses

The town's old gabled houses resemble a display of brick-coloured wedding cakes, some stepped, some with pointed ridges, some with ornate tracery and some with rounded arches, but all decorated differently: white spheres, scrolls, spirals, obelisks, garlands of flowers, horns of plenty, urns, freestanding demigods, fantastic mythical beasts, roundels, coats of arms and gilded inscriptions.

All the old gabled houses lean forward slightly. It is called 'building out of alignment' and it eases the job of the warehouseman or removal company when hoisting goods in or out of the building. Most houses are fitted with a heavy hoisting beam protruding forward from the gable.

The authorities not only stipulated the width and height of the canal-side houses but they sometimes laid down regulations about the quality of the bricks to be used. The unscrupulous builder risked having inferior building materials intercepted by inspectors at the city gates. The houses along the three main canals, however, were subject to the strictest controls and the message came over clearly to the builder: you can only build there if you can afford the best materials.

The bricklayers and carpenters who implemented the plans of the quality-conscious architects had a natural eye for beauty. The proportions were always carefully weighed up, so close attention would be paid, for example, to the distance between doors and windows.

The canal walls and the houses alongside the canals are built on piles and it is consequently very rare to find a house in Amsterdam with a cellar. Many of the old merchants' houses were divided up so that the office was on the ground floor, the private rooms were above and the goods were stored in the attic. The goods would be towed into the city from the port on barges – larger boats could not enter the canal network because of the low bridges.

Typical gabled house

A hoisting beam

A well-proportioned house

Gable styles

Over a period of 400 years, Amsterdam's designers and architects developed various gable styles. At the beginning of the 14th century, the simple, pointed, wooden gable end as seen in the Begijnhof, Houten Huis and at Zeedijk 1 was standard, but with the growing wealth of the town, the frontages became more lavishly decorated. Only warehouses retained the basic spout gable, an inverted V-shape, while rich patricians preferred the more decorative step gable on their mansions (*see Bartolotti Huis, 170 Herengracht, page 23*).

Then came the elegant neck gable, which allowed for some adornment in the triangle between the 'neck' and

Neck and shoulder gable

'shoulder'. The neck gable was adapted slightly to make the bell gable which was often finished with scrollwork. It is a common style on 18th-century houses, incorporating the clear influence of French classicism. Overflowing cornices are another architectural feature which is typical of this period.

Finally, the plain, moulded gable became popular. It resembled an architrave, often linking two houses. On some examples, the crossbeam is lightly ornamented.

Instead of house numbers, gable stones were placed above the doorways. The symbol carved in the stone revealed the profession of the person who lived there. Thus the gable stone became a firm's hallmark.

Rat Catcher gable stone

Thousands of residences and warehouses along the canals are still well preserved and need expensive maintenance. But it is no longer the rich patrician families who are footing the bill. Behind the bull's eye window panes are the busy offices of international companies. At one time imported goods from the colonies were stored in the warehouses on Prins Hendrikkade and these buildings epitomised the wealth of the city and its merchants. Now telexes and computers click and whirr.

The Hofjes

A Baedeker guide to Amsterdam published in 1880 informed its readers that the city had a number of 'charitable institutions'. It was referring to the almshouses, some of which can be described as *hofjes*.

These dwellings were originally founded for poor, old, single or lonely members of the community. The narrow houses were usually grouped around pretty, well-cared-for *hofjes* or courtyards. Access to these havens of peace was often from a small, unobtrusive doorway.

Unobtrusive hofje entrance

Most *hofjes* were established in the 17th and 18th century with the aid of donations. The Diaconiedorphofje between the Amstel and Nieuwe Prinsengracht was one such institution, bordering Weesperstraat and Nieuwe Keizersgracht. The red-brick Amstelhof is one of the most striking parts of the building. In the main hall, the first king of the Netherlands, William I, held his inaugural court ball in 1813.

Situated on the same site is the Corvershof, which was founded in 1723 by a member of the Amsterdam riflemen's guild. The original furnishings are of interest and some valuable paintings are on display in the Regent's Hall.

Behind a plain doorway in Nieuwe Keizersgracht 94 is Occo's Hofje. There is a pretty garden and a collection of Regency paintings. This Catholic almshouse was commissioned by the banker Pompejus Occo, who lived in the House of Paradise in Kalverstraat. It is claimed that he financed the king of Denmark and that his library was the envy of 16th-century Europe. Another famous *hofje* is at Amstel 86–98. Isaac Swigter, a well-known bookseller and publisher, designed and financed the construction of the houses, but insisted that only impoverished Catholic widows and spinsters should be allowed to reside in them.

The Deutzenhofje in Prinsengracht 855–99 has a pleasant atmosphere. It was commissioned by the daughter of the mayor, Agneta Deutz, and built by Steven and Jacob Vennecool. It is still owned and administered by the founder's descendants. The Regency Room here also contains some impressive works of art. At the entrance to the *hofje* is a notice which informs potential visitors that access is not allowed, but a visit may be possible if a 'polite request' is made to the caretaker.

The Hodshon-Dedelhofje in Eerste Weteringsdwarstraat was built in 1842 for staff employed by Isaac Dedel.

A little beyond is Grill's Hofje, which a Swedish couple, Anthonie and Elisabeth Grill, donated to the people of Amsterdam in recognition of their hospitality.

In the Jordaan district (*see Route 5*) there is a total of 11 *hofjes*. The Venetiehofje at Elandstraat 106–38 was built by the merchant Jacob Stoffels in the 17th century. His generous donation followed some profitable business dealings in Venice.

The recently renovated Looijershofje in Nieuwe Looijersstraat is worth a visit, as is the oldest almshouse in Amsterdam, Sint Andrieshof, at Egelantiersgracht 105–41. The latter was founded by a priest.

The delightful Bossehofje and the Rapenhofje in the Palmgracht are also worth a visit. Just a short distance away at Lindengracht 149–63, tucked away at the end of a narrow alley, is the Suykerhof, a pretty courtyard with an old water pump.

Suykerhof courtyard

In Eerste Egelantiers-Dwarsstraat, the Claes Claesz, sometimes called the Anslohofje, consists of four inner courtyards which lead into one another. Another very pretty courtyard is the Hofje Star van Brienen at Prinsengracht 85–133, opposite the Noordermarkt. The story goes that Jan van Brienen once locked himself inside his own safe and was rescued from suffocation only just in time. He showed his gratitude for his narrow escape by founding these almshouses.

Hofje Star van Brienen

A little further along Prinsengracht, at 159–71, is Zon's Hofje. The Frisian Mennonite Community in Amsterdam bought a building here called 'De Kleine Zon' (The Little Sun) in 1720. It was used as a church and renamed 'De Arke Noach' (Noah's Ark). In 1765 the church was converted into almshouses, which today provide the ultimate in secluded, tranquil living.

Rijksmuseum exhibit

Museums and Galleries

Amsterdam has 42 museums, ranging from some of Europe's finest art collections to a host of small, specialist museums reflecting the diversity of the city's culture. The top three attractions, the Rijksmuseum and the Van Gogh and Stedelijk museums, are all conveniently located round the Museumplein.

Most museums are closed on Sunday mornings and all day Monday. Admission prices vary and there are often reductions for children and groups. If you're going to be visiting a lot of museums, you may want to consider the Museumjaarkaart, the annual museum ticket which provides free access to 350 museums in Holland, 16 of them in Amsterdam. Available from the VVV Tourist Information Centres and at most museums, it represents a considerable saving if you are staying for a while and visiting other towns in Holland.

The letters MB signify that a museum can be reached by Museum Boat (*see page 88*).

Anne Frank House

Allard Pierson Museum, Oude Turfmarkt 127. Tuesday to Friday 10am–5pm, Saturday, Sunday and holidays 1–5pm. Collection of archaeological finds from Egypt, Greece, Mesopotamia and Rome. *Tram 4, 9, 14, 16, 24, 25; MB.*

Anne Frank House, Prinsengracht 263. Winter, Monday to Saturday 9am–5pm, Sunday and holidays 10am–5pm; summer, Monday to Saturday 9am–7pm, Sunday and holidays 10am–5pm. Closed for Yom Kippur. The house in which the young Jewish girl Anne Frank, author of the famous diary, sought refuge, with her family, from the Nazis during World War II. Exhibition gives background information on the war and the occupation. *Bus 21, 67; Tram 13, 14, 17; MB.*

Bijbels Museum (Bible Museum), Herengracht 366. Tuesday to Saturday 10am–5pm, Sunday and holidays 1–5pm. Biblical antiquities and ritual artefacts from the Middle East. *Tram 1, 2, 5; MB.*

De Werf't Kromhout (Shipyard Museum), Hoogte Kadijk 147. Monday to Saturday 10am–5pm, Sunday and holidays 1–5pm. Permanent exhibition of shipyard machinery in one shed, dating from 1867. Includes equipment used in boat-building, sailmaking, etc. *Bus 22, 28; Tram 7, 14; MB.*

Kromhout Museum

Electrische Museum Tramlijn (Tram Museum), Haarlemmermeerstation, Amstelveenseweg 264. 1 April to 28 October, Sunday 10am–6pm; 2 June to 1 September also Saturday noon–6pm. Rides on old tramcars (about 6km/4 miles). *Bus 15, 23, 60; Tram 6, 16.*

Historisch Museum Amsterdam (Historical Museum), Kalverstraat 92. Monday to Friday 10am–5pm, Saturday and Sunday 11am–5pm. History of the city from the 13th century to the present day. Paintings, engravings, glass, faience pottery, archaeological finds. Shooting gallery. *Tram 1, 2, 5; MB.*

Historical Museum exhibit

Informatiecentrum Ruimtelijke Ordening Zuiderkerk (Town Planning Information Centre in the Zuiderkerk), Zuiderkerkhof 72. Monday to Friday 12.30–4.30pm, Thursday also 6pm–9pm. Closed Saturday, Sunday and holidays. Future plans for the city are on view, as well as models showing its past development. *Nearest underground station: Nieuwmarkt.*

Joods Historisch Museum (Museum of Jewish History), Jonas Daniël Meijerplein 2–4. Monday to Sunday 11am–5pm. Closed for Yom Kippur. Paintings and documents on the history of Judaism in the Netherlands. *Nearest underground station: Waterlooplein; MB.*

Luchtvaartexpo Aviodome (Aeronautical Museum), Schiphol Airport. 1 October–1 May, Tuesday–Friday 10am–5pm, Saturday and Sunday noon–5pm; 2 May–30 September, Monday to Sunday 10am–5pm; air and space travel past and present. *Train from Centraal Station.*

Koninklijk Paleis (Royal Palace), Dam Square. Wednesday afternoons only, except mid-June to end of August daily 2–4pm. This is the Queen's residence when she is in Amsterdam. The finest rooms which can be visited are the Treasurer's Room, the Hall of the Aldermen and the Council Hall. *Tram 4, 9, 16, 24, 25.*

Max Euwe Centrum, Paleisstraat 1. Monday to Friday 10.30am–4pm; first Saturday in the month 10am–4.30pm. History and development of the game of chess with an account of the life of world chess master Max Euwe. *Tram 4, 9, 16, 24, 25.*

Museum Amstelkring Ons' Lieve Heer op Solder (Our Lord in the Attic), Oudezijds Voorburgwal 40. Monday to Saturday 10am–5pm, Sunday and holidays 1–5pm. Concealed church in a 17th-century merchant's home, with paintings, silver, books and engravings depicting life in Holland after the Reformation. *Bus 56; Tram 4, 9, 16, 24, 25; nearest underground station: Centraal Station or Nieuwmarkt; MB.*

Museum Fodor, Keizersgracht 609. Tuesday to Saturday 10am–5pm, Sundays and holidays 1–5pm. Art by Amsterdam artists. *Tram 1, 2, 5, 16, 24, 25; MB.*

Museum Overholland, Museumplein 4. Tuesday to Saturday 11am–5pm, Sunday and public holidays 1–5pm. Contemporary works, mainly by Dutch artists. *Tram 2, 5, 16; MB.*

Museum van Loon, Keizersgracht 672. Monday 10am–5pm, Sunday 1–5pm. Typical 17th-century canal-side house. *Tram 16, 24, 25*

Nederlands Presmuseum (Press Museum), Singel 425 (Exhibition room in the university library). Monday to Friday 10am–noon, 1–4pm. The history of the Dutch press since 1618, which includes unusual examples of both old and recent newspapers, posters, pamphlets and political cartoons by A Hahn and L J Jordaan. *Tram 1, 2, 4, 5, 9, 13, 14, 17, 24, 25.*

Dutch Maritime Museum

Outside the Rembrandthuis

Nederlands Scheepvaart Museum (Dutch Maritime Museum), Kattenburgerplein 1. Tuesday to Saturday 10am–5pm, Sunday and holidays 1–5pm. Models of historic ships, paintings, prints, illustrating Dutch maritime history. *Bus 22, 28; MB.*

Nederlands Theater Institut (Theatre Museum), Herengracht 166. Tuesday to Friday 10am–5pm, Saturday, Sunday and holidays 11am–5pm. The history of Dutch theatre is told in the 17th-century Bartolotti Huis. *Bus 21, 67; Tram 13, 14, 17; MB.*

NINT (Dutch Institute for Industry and Technology), Tolstraat 129. Monday to Friday 10am–4pm, Saturday and Sunday 1–5pm. Includes hands-on displays relating to natural science and technology. Car manufacture and shipbuilding. *Tram 4.*

Peter Stuyvesant Stichting, Drentestraat 21. Visits by prior arrangement, tel: 540 6252. Modern paintings and sculptures by well-known artists. *Bus 23, 65.*

Rembrandthuis, Jodenbreestraat 4–6. Monday to Saturday 10am–5pm, Sunday and holidays 1–5pm. Rembrandt lived here for over 20 years. Paintings, sculptures, art treasures and some personal effects. Most of the 250 etchings are on permanent display. *Tram 9, 14; nearest underground station: Waterlooplein; MB.*

Rijksmuseum (National Museum), Stadhouderskade 42. Tuesday to Saturday 10am–5pm, Sunday and holidays 1–5pm. Dutch paintings from the 15th to 19th century including masterpieces by Rembrandt, Vermeer, Frans Hals, van Ruisdael; Dutch sculpture and applied art from the 13th to 19th century; National Collection of Prints and Drawings; Museum of Asiatic Art; Library of Art History. *Bus 26, 65, 66, 67; Tram 1, 2, 5, 6, 7, 10; MB.*

Rijksmuseum Vincent van Gogh, Paulus Potterstraat 7–11. Tuesday to Saturday 10am–5pm, Sunday and holidays 1–5pm. Paintings and drawings by Van Gogh and his contemporaries (Toulouse-Lautrec, Gauguin, etc), as well as a library of letters which includes correspondence between Van Gogh and his brother Theo. *Bus 26, 65, 66, 67; Tram 2, 6, 7,10; MB.*

Spaarpottenmuseum (Money Box Museum), Raadhuisstraat 20. Monday to Friday 1–4pm. Twelve thousand different money boxes from all over the world. *Bus 21, 67; Tram 1, 2, 5, 13, 17.*

Stedelijk Museum (Municipal Museum), Paulus Potterstraat 13. Tuesday to Saturday 10am–5pm, Sunday and holidays 1–5pm. Dutch masters, 19th- and 20th-century painters; sculpture garden which includes a Henry Moore sculpture. *Bus 26, 65, 66, 67; Tram 2, 3, 5, 12; MB.*

Tropenmuseum, Linnaeusstraat 2. Monday to Friday 10am–5pm, Saturday, Sunday and holidays noon–5pm. Displays of art and everyday objects from tropical and subtropical countries. *Bus 22; Tram 3, 6, 9, 10; MB.*

Verzetsmuseum Amsterdam (Resistance Museum), Lekstraat 63. Tuesday to Friday 10am–5pm, Saturday and Sunday 1–5pm. The main theme of this museum is the Dutch resistance to the Nazi occupation during World War II, but it also deals with the issues of anti-semitism, racism and discrimination. *Bus 15; Tram 4, 12, 25.*

Werkspoorwegmuseum (Railway Museum), Oostenburgergracht 28. Open by prior arrangement, tel: 625 1035. A must for railway enthusiasts. Trains and steam engines from the 19th century. *Bus 28.*

Willet Holthuysen Museum, Herengracht 605. Tuesday to Saturday 10am–5pm, Sunday and holidays 1–5pm. Local history exhibits with furniture, glass and pottery, as well as paintings and gold jewellery from the 16th to the 19th century. *Tram 4.*

Zeiss Planetarium, Artis, Plantage-Kerklaan. Thursday to Sunday 10am–6pm, Tuesday and Wednesday 10am–8pm. Changing exhibitions on astronomy and space travel. *Tram 9, 14.*

Zoologisch Museum, Plantage Middenlaan 53. Tuesday to Friday and Sunday 9.30am–4.30pm. Interesting exhibits on the evolution of various animal species. *Tram 6, 7, 9, 10, 14.*

Rijksmuseum exhibit

In the Stedelijk Museum

Theatre and Music

With its rich cultural heritage, Amsterdam offers a varied programme of theatrical and musical events. The performances at the annual Holland Festival in June are usually of a very high standard. Details are available from Kleine Gartmanplantsoen 21, NL-1017 RP Amsterdam, tel: 020-627 6566.

A weekly listing costs NLG1 and is available from the VVV Tourist Information Centres.

Blue Bridge and Music Theatre

Concertgebouw

Concerts

The focus for music-lovers must be the famous Concertgebouw Orchestra. The concert hall with its superb acoustics is situated near the major museums in van Baerlestraat 98, tel: 671 8345 (10am–3pm) for the box office.

The Concertgebouw is not the only classical music venue. A chamber music concert is held in the Museum Amstelkring, OZ Voorburgwal 40, every month between October and May. The Bachzaal at Bachstraat 5 is the concert hall of the Amsterdam Conservatory and the students give frequent concerts. Music by contemporary composers can often be heard at de IJsbreker, Weesperzijde 23.

Organ recitals are given in several of the city's historic churches, with the Moses and Aaronkerk in Waterlooplein perhaps the best venue. It has become a centre for lovers of church music and the programme is posted on the church door.

Ballet

The Dutch Ballet Company (Nederlands Danstheater, Nationaal Ballet, Scapino) is very highly regarded. They usually perform in the Muziektheater on the Waterlooplein. Box office tel: 625 5455.

Theatre

The Theater Carré at Amstel 115 stages plays written by top-class dramatists and performed by professional actors. Box office tel: 622 5225 (10am–7pm).

There is a range of smaller theatres offering popular, contemporary and experimental drama:

Nieuwe de la Mar Theater, Marnixstraat 404.
De Brakke Grond, Nes 45.
Theater Tingel-Tangel, NZ Voorburgwal 282.
Felix Meritis, Keizersgracht 324.
Mickery (Theatre of International Experimental Theatre), Rozengracht 117.

In the summer months of July and August, the programme for the five main theatres is prepared with tourists in mind. The theatre newspaper *Uitkrant* gives details of all productions currently showing in Amsterdam. It is available from the Uit Bureau in Leidseplein 26 (Stadschouwburg), tel: 621 1211. Theatre tickets may be purchased in advance from Theater Bespreek Bureau Amsterdam at the VVV centre on the Stationsplein, tel: 626 6444, and at the Ticketshop in the Uit Bureau.

Barrel organs

One of Amsterdam's large barrel organs has returned to the Stationsplein in front of the central station. Depending on the time of year, the tunes are either slow and dignified or faster and more cheerful. Sometimes the handle is turned manually, which is not as easy as it looks, but more often an electric motor takes over the job. Whichever method is used, the *centenbakje* or brass tins are shaken vigorously in front of the passers-by. The re-emergence of these instruments has a lot to do with the current wave of nostalgia, but whole families of performers depend on them for their livelihood.

The barrel organ developed from the music box. The wood or metal cylinders could only manage one, sometimes two or occasionally three tunes, such was their limited repertoire, and the future for the street organ looked bleak. But its prospects improved dramatically at the end of the last century when a Belgian invented 'music books' for the barrel organ. Endless loops of interchangeable cardboard could punch out the tunes and, before long, barrel organ manufacturers were experiencing a revival in their fortunes. The instruments became bigger and had to be pulled by horses, but are now towed by cars. Moving figures adorn the front of these colourful boxes and their fairground music forms an ever-present soundtrack to the daily life of the city.

Nowadays, instead of asking a band to play at weddings or baptisms, many Dutch families invite a barrel organist to create a convivial atmosphere.

Shaking the centenbakje

Barrel Organ outside Centraal Station

spricht Deutsch
Engelish spoken
parle Francais

Food and Drink

Opposite: Gravenstraat restaurant

Restaurants and snack bars

The quality of meals at the gourmet-style restaurants is as high as anywhere in the world, with prices to match. Meals at mid-range restaurants are relatively expensive and the Chinese restaurants which used to represent good value are no longer quite so cheap. Around 20 of the city centre restaurants offer reasonably priced three course tourist menus at set prices. Look for the tourist menu sign in restaurant windows.

Those establishments showing signs with *Neerlands Dis* serve traditional Dutch dishes and specialities.

There is also a proliferation of foreign restaurants. The Dutch have a preference for spicy Indian and Indonesian dishes, but the opportunity also exists to try food from China, Denmark, Japan, Morocco, Mexico, Norway, Poland, Spain, Turkey, Hungary and many other countries.

Snack bar menu

For those in a hurry, there is a sandwich bar or a burger bar at almost every corner selling a wide range of tasty snacks at very reasonable prices. Although the usual international favourites such as hamburgers and pizzas are readily available, many Dutch people would recommend the delicious fresh bread rolls with a variety of different fillings which are sold in the *broodjeswinkels*.

Another local favourite are the numerous pancake restaurants. Children will love them but they are also very popular with adults.

The VVV Tourist Information Centre issues a very useful, inexpensive booklet entitled 'Eating and Drinking in Amsterdam'.

Café interior

Cafés

In the city centre canal area, there are over 400 cafés but the term 'café' does not really do them justice. These popular meeting places are more than just somewhere for a cup of coffee and a cake, as they also sell alcoholic drinks and have much in common with the English pub. Families are usually welcome and there is always a warm and friendly atmosphere.

A canal-side café

The so-called *bruin cafés* with their brown painted walls and ceilings stained with tobacco smoke are usually the haunt of students, journalists and actors, although tourists are always welcome. Each café will have regular customers, who appreciate its particular character: musical evenings perhaps, or literary soirées. There are so many different cafés, each with their own clientele, that it is impossible to list them all, but any visitor to the city ought to take the opportunity to call in at a few of them for a beer, as they have great charm and character and are something that is unique to Amsterdam.

Drie Fleschjes taster bar

Taster bars

The friendly taster bars or *proeflokale* are another typical Amsterdam institution. They are popular places for Amsterdammers who like to meet there late in the afternoon on the way home from work and chat over a glass of *jenever* (gin). They usually close at around 8pm.

Wine

Continental Bodega, Lijnbaansgracht 246.

Spirits

Bols Taverne, Rozengracht 106.
Hoppe, Spui 18.
De Drie Fleschjes, Gravenstraat 18.

Liquor shop in Spuistraat

Consumer information

All cafés and bars are obliged to display notices giving details of how drinks will be served, so the customer knows what to expect:

Volledige vergunning: all drinks are served in a glass or as a full bottle.

Tapvergunning: all drinks are served in a glass.

Verlof A: only low-alcohol drinks such as beer and wine are served.

Terminology for the drinker

amerikaantje: beer with framboise (raspberry liqueur)
bakkie: a large beer
graantje: a small beer
kabouterpils: a small pils
koetsiertje: Dutch brandy
oortje: a glass of jenever (gin)
spanjooltje: gin with blackcurrant.

A taste to savour

Shopping

The VVV Tourist Information Centres supply brochures on some of the most interesting shops in Amsterdam. For a small charge, booklets are available in English which give further information on specialist areas, such as art and antiques, Jordaan and the shops 'between the canals'.

Art and antiques

There are a great many art dealers and antique shops in the area around Spiegelgracht and Nieuwe Spiegelstraat on the town centre side of the Rijksmuseum. But a stroll around the canal and the nearby streets will certainly lead you to other antique shops. Some of the most reputable dealers are in the Rokin.

For further information contact the Vereeniging van Handelaren in Oude Kunst (Association of Art Dealers), Keizersgracht 708, tel: 623 8904.

Antique shop

Auctions

There are three internationally renowned auction houses in Amsterdam:

Paul Brandt, Keizersgracht 738, tel: 624 8662.
Sotheby/Mak van Waay, Rokin 102, tel: 624 6215
Christie's Kunstveilingen, Cornelis Schuytstraat 57, tel: 664 2011.

Auctions take place throughout the year apart from during the summer months. Days are set aside for viewing and these can prove very interesting. The excellent catalogues also make fascinating reading.

Modern art

There are a number of small art galleries in the canal district:

Jaski Art Galerie, Nieuwe Spiegelstraat 27.
Galerie Swart, Van Breestraat 23.
Collection d'Art, Keizersgracht 516.
Galerie Espace, Keizersgracht 548.
Galerie Krikhaar, Spuistraat 330
Galerie Petit, NZ Voorburgwal 270.

Art gallery attracts attention

Flea market

The best-known flea market in Amsterdam is held in Waterlooplein (daily except Sunday 10am–5pm, *see page 36*).

Antiques markets

The flea market on the Waterlooplein (*see above*) is well worth a visit, but for those genuinely interested in antiques the **De Looier** antiques and bric-à-brac markets in the Elendsgracht 109 (Saturday to Wednesday 11am–5pm, Thursday 11am–9pm) are probably more worthwhile.

There is another antiques market on the Spui (every Friday 10am–6pm).

Art market

Thorbeckeplein (May to October, Sunday).

Other markets

General goods including food, clothing, household goods, flowers, etc:
Albert Cuypstraat (daily except Sunday).
Dapperstraat (Tuesday to Saturday).
Ten Katestraat (daily except Sunday and Monday).

Singel flower market

Flower market
Singel (daily except Sunday).
Amstelveld (Monday only 10am–noon).
Stamp and coin market
NZ Voorburgwal behind the Royal Palace (Wednesday and Saturday 9am–1pm).
Fabrics (Lapjesmarkt)
Noordermarkt (Monday).
Westerstraat (Monday morning).
Bird market
Noordermarkt (Saturday morning).

Diamond workshop sign

Diamonds

Amsterdam is an important diamond centre and a number of diamond cutting workshops may be visited. These workshops will sell small, perfect diamonds to private individuals. If a bigger stone is purchased at a later date, the dealer will usually agree to buy back the smaller diamond at the original price.
Stoeltie, Wagenstraat 13–17.
Diamant Industrie A. van Moppes & Zoon, Albert Cuypstraat 2–6.
Coster Diamond, Paulus Potterstraat 2.
Amsterdam Diamond Center, Rokin 1.
Samual Gassan, Nieuwe Achtergracht 17–23.

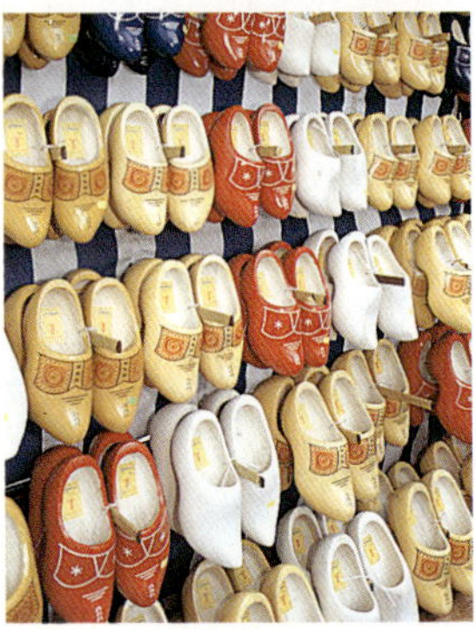

Clogs for sale

Amsterdam specialities

Clogs: De Klompenboer, NZ Voorburgwal 20, specialises in the manufacture and sale of Dutch clogs.

Pearls: A. Copenhagen, Bloemgracht 38 are one of the foremost pearl specialists

Wys & Zn. Coffee Shop: Warmoestraat 102. Buying coffee here is a pleasure. Unusual containers and traditional décor.

Liquorice: Jacob Hooy, Kloveniersburgwal 12, is the oldest herbalist in the city, with a wide range of licorice.

Delftware

Pottery and china: Focke & Meltzer, Rokin 124, are established suppliers of Delftware. Makkum pottery is also worth investigating.

Pipes: Cheap clay pipes and also the most expensive brands in the world are on sale at Hajenius, Rokin 92.

Glazed tiles: Eduard Kramer, Nieuwe Spiegelstraat 64, undoubtedly has the widest selection.

Shopping centres

The following are pedestrian precincts: Nieuwendijk, Kalverstraat, Heiligeweg, Leidsestraat and the Winkelcentrum (Amsterdam-Noord).

The following are major shopping streets: Damrak, Rokin, Regulierbreestraat, Elendsgracht, Van Baerlestraat, Beethovenstraat and Gelderlandplein.

Department stores

On the corner of the Damrak and Dam Square is De Bijenkorf. This large department store has been in business for 120 years and has a nationwide reputation for high quality goods.

At Kalverstraat 183, the Maison de Bonneterie, another long-established store, occupies one of the best sites in the city centre. Before the recent opening of a branch of Harrods, the fortunes of this old shopping street had started to decline, but it has now recovered something of its once-fashionable reputation.

At NZ Voorburgwal 182, the old post office which dated from 1899 has undergone a transformation and the neo-Gothic building now houses the Magna Plaza, a magnificent, new shopping centre. There are shops selling a range of goods from sports equipment to fashions, fashion accessories and cosmetics.

Finally, no trip to Amsterdam is complete without a visit to Metz & Co on the corner of Keizersgracht and Leidsestraat. The view from the roof restaurant shows Amsterdam at its best.

Fashion boutique

No shortage of souvenirs

Added Attractions

Family-sized bike

Bell ringing

Koninklijk Paleis, Dam Square (Monday noon–1pm).
Oude Kerk, Ouderkerksplein (Saturday 4–5pm).
Munttoren, Muntplein (Tuesday and Friday 12.30–1pm).
Westerkerk, Westermarkt (Tuesday noon–1pm).
Zuiderkerk, Zandstraat (Thursday noon–1pm).

Church towers

Oude Kerk, Ouderkerksplein (1 June–15 September, Monday–Saturday 10am–5pm).
Westerkerk, Westermarkt (1 June–15 September, Tuesday, Wednesday, Friday, Saturday 2–5pm).

Amsterdam for children

Amsterdam is a city with many attractions for young people. Children will find a tour of the canals much more fun if their parents hire a waterbike (*see page 89*).

In Madame Tussaud's

Both children and adults will enjoy **Madame Tussaud's Panopticum** in Kalverstraat 156. It is the only Madame Tussaud's outside London (daily from 10am).

The Rijksmuseum houses a collection of patrician houses in miniature. Older children may well be interested in the Dutch Maritime Museum (*see page 70*).

The VVV Tourist Information Centres can provide additional details on the **Tram Museum** at Haarlemmermeerstation (tram 6 and 16), where at weekends between April and September old tramcars take visitors on 6-km (4-mile) rides into the Amsterdamse Bos.

Other places which will interest children are:

Diridas puppet theatre, Hobbemakade 68. Wednesday, Saturday and Sunday afternoons.

Circus Elleboog, Passeedergracht 32. First and third Saturday and Sunday afternoons in the month.

De Krakeling, Nieuwe Passeerdersstraat 1. A lively youth theatre.

Artis Zoo with planetarium and zoological museum, Plantage Middenlaan 40. Daily from 9am.

A separate department of the Tropenmuseum (*see page 71*) is the children's museum **Kindermuseum TM Junior**, exclusively geared towards children aged 6 to 12.

Flowers for auction

Other places of interest

Aquarium near Artis Zoo, Plantage Middenlaan 53.
Flower Auction, Aalsmeer, Legmeerdijk 313.
University Botanical Gardens, Plantage Middenlaan 2 and Boechorststraat 8.
Film Museum, Paviljoen Vondelpark, Vondelpark 3.
Amsterdamse Bos (Amsterdam Wood) Museum, Amstelveenseweg 264.

Nightlife

Evening canal scene

Jazz fans will find the following establishments well worth visiting:

BIMhuis, Oude Schans 73–7; Joseph Lam Jazzclub, Laagte Kadijk 35; De Kroeg Lijnbaansgracht 163; Cab Kaye's Jazzpiano Bar, Beulingstraat 9.

Regular jazz nights are also held in Paradiso and Melkweg (*see page 91*).

Classical entrance in Damrak

Cinema

All foreign films are shown with subtitles. The starting times of performances varies but, as a general rule, matinées start at 2pm. Sometimes the last performance starts as late as 10pm.

The Tuschinski Film Theatre at Reguliersbreestraat 26 is worth a visit if only for its splendidly preserved art nouveau décor.

Nightclubs

Amsterdam's nightclubs do not quite enjoy the same reputation for chic and refinement as those in many other European major cities. The so-called floor shows certainly do not live up to international standards, but prices reflect this, as they are not very high. The majority of nightclubs and bars are in the Rembrandtsplein, Thorbeckeplein and Leidseplein area. The **Pink Elephant** at Thorbeckeplein 6–10 is currently one of the most popular venues.

Well-stocked bar

Closing time

Most establishments close around 1am, but in the Leidseplein, Rembrandtsplein, Zeedijk and Warmoestraat area many of the bars stay open until 2am and until 3am on Friday and Saturday.

TAXI

Getting There

By plane

Schipol Airport, arguably Europe's most popular international airport, is situated 18km (11 miles) from Amsterdam city centre. Trains to and from the airport leave every 15 minutes. Schipol is served by most major airlines. The national carrier is KLM Royal Dutch Airlines, which has flights from most UK airports (tel: 0181 750 9000), and from many airports in North America (tel: 1-800 374 7747).

By rail

There are direct rail connections from all over Europe and seats can be reserved on the comfortable EuroCity trains. Day and night services operate from London (Liverpool Street) to Amsterdam via the Hook of Holland – a journey time of around 12 hours by ferry, 10 hours by jetfoil. A quicker option is London (Victoria) to Ostend via Dover, but there are several transfers involved. You can also go by the Sheerness to Vlissingen rail ferry.

The Eurostar Channel Tunnel train (tel: 44-1233 617575 from abroad; 0345 881 881 from within the UK) links London to Brussels in three hours, from where there are fast connections to destinations in Holland. There are good rail connections to Amsterdam from the main ports of arrival. Amsterdam's railway station, the impressive Centraal Station at Stationsplein, has excellent connections to the rest of the country and a very regular service to Brussels, Paris, Antwerp, Cologne and Hanover.

The Holland Rail Pass gives travellers three days of unlimited travel on Dutch railways within a period of 15 days. Children between the age of 4 and 11 get considerable reductions and the Benelux Tourrail Junior is available for young people aged between 12 and 25.

Good rail connections

Centraal Station

By sea

Sealink operates two sailings a day from Harwich to the Hook of Holland: crossing time 7 hours by day, 8 hours at night. North Sea Ferries has a daily sailing from Hull to Rotterdam, taking 14 hours, useful for visitors from the north of England. Olau Line, which has a reputation for the highest standards, has two sailings a day from Sheerness to Vlissingen, taking 7 hours by day, 8 hours by night.

The fastest sea route from the UK is the jetfoil from Dover to Ostend.

An alternative for motorists is Le Shuttle, the Channel Tunnel service taking cars and their passengers from Folkestone to Calais on a drive-on-drive-off system. The journey through the tunnel takes 35 minutes; from Calais there are fast motorway connections up to Holland.

Parking near the station

By car

Except for the jetfoil service, all the companies mentioned on the previous page offer a car ferry service. The journey from the Hook of Holland takes about 3.5 hours. The ANWB in The Hague, tel: 070 331 3131, runs a traffic information service which includes roadworks, congestion and weather reports for the international road network as well as Holland.

The maximum speed limit in built-up areas is 50km/h (31mph), outside towns the limit is 80km/h (50mph) and on motorways the limit is 120km/h (75mph). Motorists should remember to display a nationality sticker clearly on the rear of the car. It is generally unwise to travel by car into the centre of Amsterdam as parking is difficult and expensive. The radial roads leading into Amsterdam are the city's main arteries but they have only a limited capacity, so there is always a risk of serious congestion.

Many people suffer a great deal of inconvenience and cost through parking in the wrong place. The Amsterdam traffic police can have a car clamped or towed away within 10 minutes. Offenders can expect to pay a hefty fine in order to reclaim their car; contact the traffic police, tel:627 5877.

Traffic information: ANWB offices: Museumsplein 5, tel: 673 0844, Monday to Friday 8.45am–4.15pm, Saturday 8.45am–noon.

Breakdowns: The yellow vans of the ANWB (roadside assistance) patrol all the main roads into Amsterdam between 7am and midnight. To call for help at any time of the day, tel: 06 08 88. The number for Amsterdam's breakdown service is 626 8251.

A picturesque parking spot

Getting Around

Parking

Parking on the pavement is not permitted and very often impossible, as the city centre canal area has been 'planted' with the notorious *amsterdammertjes* (bollards).

For those who are staying in the inner city area, the best advice is to find a spot for your car and leave it there, even if it means a long search. A car is not really necessary in this compact city. Three-day parking permits can be purchased from some hotels. Permits for one or several days can also be purchased from kiosks. They are not cheap, but they enable you to park anywhere in the city. Ask at your hotel or a tourist centre for the nearest kiosk. Take care when parking alongside the canals as the low barriers are not absolutely reliable blockades.

Car parks in the inner city: Bijenkorf, Beursplein (open until 6pm and closed on Sunday); Europarking, Marnixstraat 250; Hirsch-Gebouw, Leidsekade (near the Lido); Krasnopolsky, St Jansstraat; Rai, Europa Boulevard; Museumsplein, entrance in Gabriel Metsusstraat; Muziektheater, Waterlooplein.

Car park on the underground: Bijlmer, Diemen-Zuid, Gaasperplas.

Car parks on the edge of the city: Buikslotermeerplein (Amsterdam-Noord, Nieuwendam), bus 32 and 33; Flevoparkbad, Zuiderzeeweg (Amsterdam-Oost), bus 22, tram 10.

Parking instructions

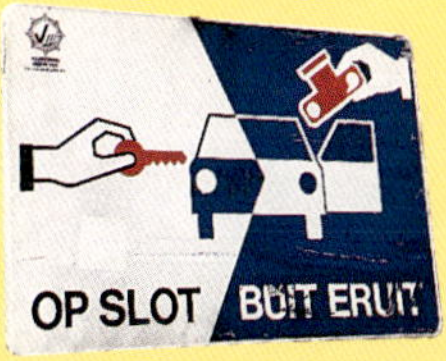

Cyclists' city

Cyclists

This is a city of cyclists and many visitors bring their own bicycles. Nearly all roads outside the city centre have special cycleways. Note that the lower part of the rear mudguard must be painted white, although cyclists are not always obliged to adhere to the rules regarding one-way streets.

It is also possible to hire bikes, *fiets* in Dutch, from the following firms:

Fiets-o-fiets, Amstelveenseweg 880–900, tel: 644 5473.

Damstraat Rent-a-bike, P J Dwarsstraat 11, tel: 625 5029.

Koenders Rent-a-bike, Stationsplein 33 (near the central station), tel: 624 8391.

For guided tours of the city by bike: Yellow Bike, NZ Voorburgwal 66, tel: 620 6940.

Bikes for hire

Public transport

See map, pages 86–7. There are 16 tram routes, around 30 bus routes and two underground lines, all of which operate from 6am to midnight. For public transport purposes, the city is divided into tariff zones.

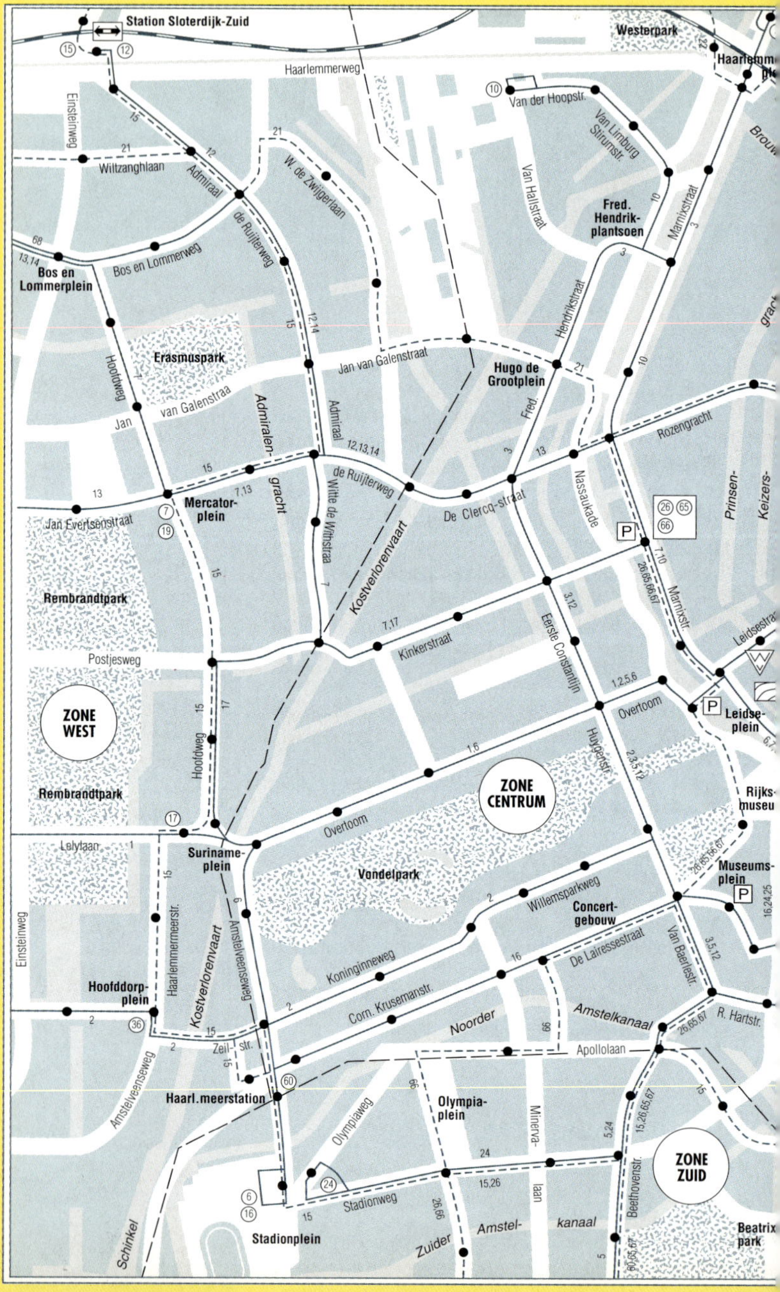
Station Sloterdijk-Zuid
Westerpark
Haarlemmerweg
Van der Hoopstr.
Van Limburg Stirumstr.
Einsteinweg
Wiltzanghlaan
Admiraal
W. de Zwijgerlaan
Van Hallstraat
Fred. Hendrik-plantsoen
Marnixstraat
de Ruijterweg
Bos en Lommerplein
Bos en Lommerweg
Hendrikstraat
Erasmuspark
Jan van Galenstraat
Hugo de Grootplein
Hoofdweg
Jan
van Galenstraa
Admiralen-gracht
Admiraal
Fred.
Rozengracht
Nassaukade
Prinsen-
Keizers-
Mercator-plein
de Ruijterweg
Witte de Withstraat
De Clercq-straat
Jan Evertsenstraat
Kostverlorenvaart
Marnixstr.
Rembrandtpark
Kinkerstraat
Eerste Constantijn
Leidsestraat
Postjesweg
Overtoom
Leidse-plein
ZONE WEST
Hoofdweg
Huygenstr.
Rembrandtpark
ZONE CENTRUM
Rijks-museu
Overtoom
Lelylaan
Suriname-plein
Vondelpark
Museums-plein
Willemsparkweg
Concert-gebouw
Einsteinweg
Haarlemmermeerstr.
Kostverlorenvaart
Amstelveenseweg
De Lairessestraat
Van Baerlestr.
Koninginneweg
Hoofddorp-plein
Corn. Krusemanstr.
Amstelkanaal
R. Hartstr.
Noorder
Zeil-str.
Apollolaan
Amstelveenseweg
Haarl.meerstation
Olympiaweg
Olympia-plein
Minerva-laan
Beethovenstr.
ZONE ZUID
Stadionweg
Schinkel
Stadionplein
Zuider
Amstel-
kanaal
Beatrix park

Buses
Trams
Underground
Railway
Zone Divisions
Information and tickets
Tourist Association
Stations
Car Parks
ZONE NOORD
ZONE OOST
Van der Pekstraat
Meeuwenlaan
IJ
De Ruijterkade
Centraalstation
Haarlemmer Houttunen
Herengracht
Singel
Damrak
Nieuwe Kerk
Dam
Rokin
O.Z. Voorburgwal
O.Z. Achterburgwal
Kloveniers-
burgwal
Oude Schans
Kattenburgerstraat
Kadijksplein
Kattenb. Gracht
Wittenb. Gracht
Oostenb. Gracht
Czaar Peterstraat
Mr. Visser-
plein
Artis Zoo
Plantage Middenlaan
N.Z. Voorburgwal
Munt-
plein
Rembrandts-
plein
Heren-
gracht
Keizers-
gracht
Prinsen-
gracht
Vijzelstraat
Utrechtsestraat
Reguliersgracht
Frederiks-
plein
Sarphartistraat
Roetersstraat
Mauritskade
Linnaeusstraat
Muiderpoort-
station
Oosterpark
schans
Stadhouderskade
Albert Cuypstraat
Sarphatipark
Ruyschstraat
Fred.
Bolstr.
Ceintuur-
baan
Van Woustraat
Weesperzijde
AMSTEL
Amsteldijk
Krugerplein
Amstelkanaal
Rijnstraat
James Wattstr.
Kamerlingh Onneslaan
Mr. Treublaan
Pr. Bernhard
plein
Amstelstation
Hugo de Vrieslaan
Vrijheidslaan
Victorie-
plein
Scheldestr.
Schelde-
plein
Europaplein
Rooseveltlaan

The strippenkaart system

Tram

These tickets work out cheaper than buying individual tickets. Tram and bus drivers sell 15-strip tickets and there are reductions for children under 10.

All types of strip-tickets are available from the GVB office (for address, *see below*) and from post offices, and are slightly cheaper than those sold on trams and buses.

The system works on a zonal basis, whereby two strips are cancelled for one zone, three strips for two and so on. Inside one zone, passengers may change as many times as they wish within one hour.

Day tickets

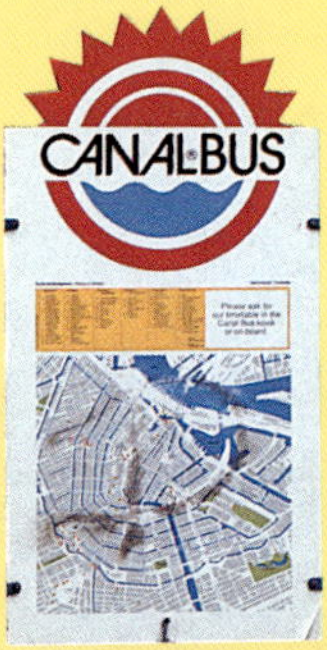

For visitors who are in the city for just one day, then the *dagkaart* or day ticket is usually the cheapest way of using the public transport system. It is valid on buses, trams and the underground for one day only and may be purchased from bus and tram drivers.

Two- three- and four-day tickets are also available. When using the ticket for the first time, it should be stamped either by the bus driver or in the yellow machine on a tram. Day tickets are available from machines at underground stations, tobacco or newspaper kiosks, as well as from the GVB kiosk at the central station by the VVV information centre (Monday–Friday 7am–10.30pm, Saturday and Sunday 8am–10.30pm).

Canal boats

Canal bus

Shuttle service

These are boats which operate a shuttle service between the central station (from the jetty near the VVV Information Centre) and the Rijksmuseum. Boats leave approximately every 45 minutes, stopping only three times on each journey. Tickets are sold on board.

The Museum Boat

Many of Amsterdam's museums are situated on or near the water. The museum boat offers a shuttle service which links all these museums together. It is an ideal opportunity for museum lovers to combine their visits with a trip along the famous canals. The museum boat has five stops to enable you to visit 20 museums and other tourist attractions. A day ticket also entitles you to reduced entrance to various museums. Available from the VVV information centre, a combination ticket covers the cost of transport and entry into three museums of your choice.

Amsterdam taxi

Taxis

It can be difficult to find a taxi at busy times. Either phone the main taxi office, tel: 6 77 77 77, or the local taxi stands at the following places:

Centraal Station (tel: 626 6103).
Dam Square (tel: 626 6104).
Leidseplein (tel: 626 6101).
Rembrandtsplein (tel: 626 6106).
Frederiksplein (tel: 626 6100).
Concertgebouw (tel: 672 9099).
Spui (tel: 626 6105).
Westermarkt (tel: 626 6102).

Although it can be quite an expensive way to travel, there is also a water taxi service which takes up to seven people (tel: 621 21 1).

City tours by boat, bus and waterbike

A tour of the canals is an essential part of a visit to Amsterdam. The journey lasts about an hour and takes in all the most interesting sights.

The boats leave from the central station, the Damrak, the Rokin, the Amstel, Nassaukade, from opposite Overtoom and from the Stadhouderskade opposite the Adda Parkhotel.

Buying tickets

Most tours follow a route along the Singel, the Herengracht to the Amstel, through the Oude Schans and into the eastern part of Amsterdam's harbour. Since the decline in the importance of Amsterdam as a port, there is now little of interest in this part of the city. Normally a commentary is given in several languages, including English, pointing out the places of interest.

Boat tour

Night cruises along the illuminated canals can be a romantic way to spend an evening.

There are also bus tours of the city covering not just the old city centre but also the suburbs. Further details can be provided by the VVV Information Centres.

There is also a tourist tram. It runs from April to the beginning of September (10.30am–4.30pm) and takes in all the main places of interest around the city.

For the more energetic visitor, waterbikes offer a degree of freedom and independence. They can be hired with seats for two or four from the following landing-stages:

Leidsebosje (near the Leidseplein) between the Rijksmuseum and the Heineken brewery.

Prinsengracht (near the Westerkerk).

Keizersgracht (on the corner of Leidsestraat).

Zeilmakerij Roëll, Mauritskade 1 (near Amstel Hotel).

Excursions

The VVV Tourist Centres offer a wide range of excursions including tours of Marken-Volendam, The Hague and Delft, the tulip fields and Keukenhof (April and May), the cheese market in Alkmaar, the windmills at Zaanse Schans and the flower auctions at Aalsmeer. Further details are available from the VVV, Stationsplein 10, tel: 626 6444.

Tourist Information Office at Centraal Station

This way for information

Facts for the Visitor

Visas
Visitors from the EU, US, Canada, Australia, New Zealand and most other European and Commonwealth countries do not require a visa.

Customs
Non-EU members can bring in 400 cigarettes, one bottle of spirits, two of wine and 50g of perfume; EU members have guide levels of 800 cigarettes, 10 litres of spirit and 90 litres of wine.

Flower bulbs
Most countries do not permit the importation of flower bulbs, unless accompanied by a document proving that they are free from disease. Tourists are therefore advised not to buy bulbs, but to order them from a specialist.

Information
In the UK: information may be obtained by writing to the Netherlands Board of Tourism, PO Box 523, London SW1E 6NT, tel: 0891 200277, fax: 0171-828 7941.
In the USA: Netherlands Board of Tourism, 355 Lexington Avenue, New York, NY10017, tel: 0212 370 7367.
In Canada: Netherlands Board of Tourism, 25 Adelaide St East, Suite 710, Ontario M5C 1YZ, tel: 0416 363 1577

In Amsterdam: VVV Stationsplein 10 (Netherlands Tourist Office café on Centraal Station concourse), tel: 626 6444. Open Easter to 30 June and September, Monday to Saturday 9am–11pm, Sunday 10am–5pm; July and August, daily 9am–11pm; October to Easter, Monday to Saturday 9am–5pm, Sunday 10am–1pm and 2–5.30pm.

VVV Leidsestraat 106. Open Easter to 30 September, Monday to Saturday 9am–8.30pm; 1 October to Good Friday, 10.30am–7pm, Saturday 10.30am–6.30pm, Sunday 10.30am–5.30pm.

VVV Rijksweg A2. Open Easter to 30 September, daily 10.30am–2pm and 2.30–6.30pm.

City Information Service, Town Hall, Waterlooplein, tel: 624 1111.

Amsterdam for young people

An information sheet called *Use It* is available free from VVV Tourist Information Centres.

Meeting places

Akhnaton, Nieuwezijdskolk 25, tel: 624 3396. Free youth centre offering a wide range of activities (5–9pm).

Dam Square in front of the Royal Palace is a favourite meeting place. Sitting (but not sleeping) on the steps of this national monument is permitted.

Kosmos Meditation Centre, Prins Hendrikkade 142, tel: 626 7477. Yoga, meditation, etc. Phone for opening times.

Melkweg, Lijnbaansgracht 243a, tel: 624 1777. Various activities including theatre and film nights. Jam sessions (Wednesday evenings), workshops, etc. (7.30pm–1am, weekends 7.30pm–2am). No events take place on Mondays and Tuesdays.

Moses and Aaronkerk, Waterlooplein 57, tel: 622 1305. Meditation room. Tea stand in the summer months.

Paradiso, Weteringschans 6–8, tel: 626 4521. This former church has become a centre for alternative culture. Events range from music to protest meetings.

Vondelpark is a different venue for young people who find Dam Square unfriendly, but sleeping rough on the lawns is not permitted.

Congregating on Dam Square

Currency and exchange

The Dutch unit of currency is the guilder (NLG). 100 cents = 1 guilder. There are banknotes in circulation for 1000, 250, 100, 50, 25 and 10 guilders and the coins are in denominations of 5, 2.50, 1 guilders and 0.25, 0.10 and 0.05 cents. The 2.50 cent coins are usually referred to as *rijksdaalder*, 25 cents are *kwartje*, 10 cents are *dubbeltje* and 5 cents are *stuiver*. It is easy to confuse the NLG5 coin with the 0.05 cent coin. Shops usually round amounts up or down to the nearest 5 cents.

There is no limit to the amount of Dutch guilders which can be exchanged back into sterling or other currency. Banks are generally open from Monday to Friday 9am–4pm; Thursday 9am–7pm. At the central station, the bureau de change is open Monday to Saturday, 7am–11pm, Sunday 8am–11pm.

Cheese salesmen

Souvenir clog

Souvenirs

Clogs either in miniature or tailor-made are a favourite souvenir of Holland as is Delft or Makkum pottery, but take care that they bear a genuine hallmark. Other souvenirs include long clay pipes from Gouda, clogs, dolls in traditional costume, biscuits, Haagse *hopjes* and *dropjes* (sweet or salty liquorice), *jenever* (gin), cheese or a diamond – as long as it carries a certificate of purity.

Tipping

The prices on restaurant menus always include service and VAT, but a tip of around 10 percent is always appreciated.

Time

The Netherlands is six hours ahead of US Eastern Standard Time and one ahead of Greenwich Mean Time.

Opening times

On weekdays most shops open from 8.30am until 5.30 or 6pm. On Saturday, they close at 5pm, but on Thursday many shops stay open until 9pm. Some shops close for lunch between 1 and 2pm. Department stores open at 10.30am on Monday and close each day at 5.30pm.

Public holidays

The following days are public holidays: New Year's Day; Good Friday (shops are usually open all day); 30 April, Queen's Day (shops are usually open in the morning); 5 May, Liberation Day (most shops are open all day); Ascension Day; Whitsuntide and Christmas Day.

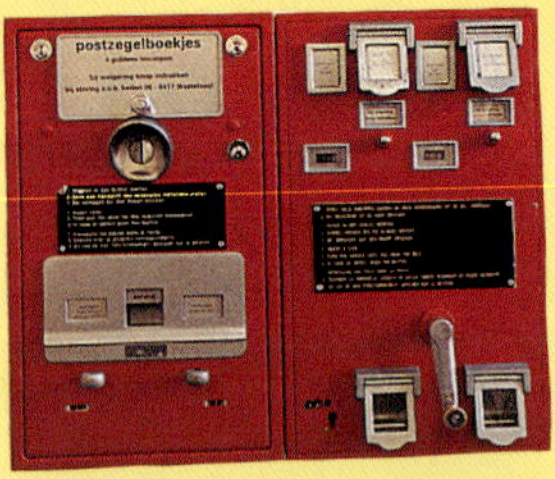

Postbox in the Historical Museum

Postal services

Post offices are open Monday to Friday 8.30am–6pm. Urgent letters may be posted on Saturdays from 9am to noon at the General Post Office on the Singel 250–6.

Telegrams may also be sent from there at any time of day. Use the entrance in Spuistraat. One counter in the General Post Office issues special Dutch stamps.

A four-language guide to postal and telephone charges is available from the VVV Tourist Information Centres, post offices and larger hotels.

Parcels should be handed in at the post office in Oosterdokskade, weekdays 8.30am–9pm, Saturday 9am–noon.

Stamps are available from post offices, tobacconists, newsstands and stamp machines attached to the red and grey letter boxes.

Public phone boxes

Telephone

Telephone boxes are green and take 25c and 1and 2.50 guilder coins. You find them in the post offices, large stores, cafés and in some streets. Blue telephones require a pre-paid telecard which can be purchased at Primafoon stores, train stations, post offices, VVV offices and selected shops. Telecards are available for 5, 10 and 25 guilders. For international calls, it may be easier to go to the Telehuis, Raadhuisstraat 48 (open 24 hours), where you can talk in a booth for as long as you like and pay later. To make an international call, dial 00 + the country code: Australia 61; France 33; Germany 49; Japan 81; Spain 34; United Kingdom 44; US and Canada 1. AT&T code: 06-022 9111. Sprint code:06-022 9119.

Medical assistance

For citizens of the EU, the Netherlands provides free medical treatment and prescribed medicine. Presentation of an E111 form obtainable from your own social security office is sufficient. Visitors from outside the EU are advised to take out their own private travel insurance policy.

Hospitals and first aid: For urgent medical help, including doctors, dentists and chemists: tel: 664 2111.

Academisch Ziekenhuis V. U., de Boelelaan 1117, tel: 5489 1117.

Academisch Medisch Centrum, Bullewijk (Bijlmermeer), tel: 566 9111.

Emergencies

Police: tel: 622 2222. The police station in Warmoestraat 44–6 covers the inner city area, tel: 559 2203.

Accidents: The 24-hour number to call in the event of an accident is tel: 555 5555.

Fire Brigade: In case of fire or if a car falls into a canal, tel: 621 2121.

Lost property: Waterlooplein 11, tel: 559 8005.

Theft: Contact the Tourist Assistance Service if passports or travellers' cheques are stolen. Nieuwezijds Voorburgwal 114 (near the Nieuwe Kerk).

Die Poort Van Cleve Hotel

Accommodation

Every year Amsterdam's Tourist Information Centre (VVV) publishes an up-to-date list of accommodation and makes the list available through the national tourist offices abroad (*see page 90*) as well as from the VVV in Amsterdam (*see page 90–1*).

The small selection of hotels listed below are categorised from **$$$$$** (about 200 dollars a night) for luxury accommodation, to **$$** (about 60 dollars a night) for a good but much more basic hotel. There are also a great many guesthouses in the city which charge much less – about 30–40 dollars a night, in a double room. Hotel prices nearly always include breakfast.

Rooms may be booked through the Nationaal Reserverings Centrum (NRC). There is no charge for the reservation but receipt of the confirmation may take a few days to arrive. Information: Nationaal Reserverings Centrum, Postbus 404, NL-2260 AK Leidschendam, tel: 31 70-320 2500, fax: 31 70-320 2611.

Restaurant in the American Hotel

$$$$$

Amstel, Professor Tulpplein 1, tel: 226060; **Apollo**, Apollolaan 2, tel: 730333; **Europe**, Nieuwe Doelenstraat 2–8, tel: 234836; **Golden Tulip Barbizon Palace**, Prins Hendrikkade 59–72, tel: 556 4564; **Okura Amsterdam**, Ferdinand Bolstraat 333, tel: 787111; **Sonesta**, Kattengat 1, tel: 212223.

$$$$

American, Leidsekade 97, tel: 245322; **Ascot**, Damrak 95–8, tel: 260066; **Krasnapolsky**, Dam 9, tel: 554 9111; **Pulitzer**, Prinsengracht 315–31, tel: 228333.

$$$

Abassade, Herengracht 341, tel: 262333; **Arthur Frommer**, Noorderstraat 46, tel: 220328; **Atlas**, Van Eeghenstraat 64, tel: 766336; **Beethoven**, 43 Beethovenstraat, tel: 664 4816; **Canal House**, Keizersgracht 148, tel: 225182; **Estherea**, Singel 303–9, tel: 245146; **Holland**, PC Hoofstraat 162, tel: 764253; **Jan Luyken**, Jan Luykenstraat 58, tel: 764111; **Museum**, PC Hoofstraat 2, tel: 831811; **Prizen**, Vondelstraat 38, tel: 162323; **Owl**, Roemer Visscherstraat 1, tel: 189484; **Terdam**, Tesselschadestraat 23, tel: 126876; **Trianon**, JW Brouwerstraat 3–7, tel: 732073; **Weichman**, Prinsengracht 328–30, tel: 263321.

Doorman at the Krasnopolsky

$$

Acro, Jan Luykenstraat 44, tel: 662 0526; **Cok Budget**, Koninginneweg 34–6, tel: 664 6111; **Quentin**, Leidsekade 89, tel: 262187; **Wijnnoble**, Vossiusstraat 9, tel: 622298.

Self-catering accommodation

Details of holiday homes and flats in and around Amsterdam are also available from the NRC or the VVV Tourist Information Centres.

Camp sites

Amsterdamse Bos, Klein Noorddijk 1, NL-1432 CC Aalsmeer, tel: 641 6868. Open 1 April to 1 November. Well-equipped camp-site with 350 pitches. *Bus CN 171, 172 from the Centraal Station.*

Amsterdamse IJsclub, IJsbaanpad 45, NL-1076 CV Amsterdam, tel: 662 0916. Open 15 March to 1 October. Good camp site with 575 pitches. *Tram 16, 24 from the Centraal Station.*

Eurocamping De Badhoeve, Uitdammerdijk 10, NL-1026 CP Amsterdam-Kinselmeer, tel: 0 29 0494. Open all year. Well-equipped camp site with 300 pitches. *Bus 30 from the Centraal Station.*

Gaaspercamping, Loosdrechtdreef 7, NL-1108 AZ Amsterdam, tel: 696 7326. Open all year. Well-equipped camp site with 750 pitches. *Nearest underground station: Gaasperplas (from the Centraal Station).*

Camp sites for young tourists

The following sites cater specifically to young people:

Camping Zeeburg, Zuider IJdijk 34A, NL-1095 KJ Amsterdam, tel: 694 4430. Open 5 April to 1 October. Basic camp site with 600 pitches. *Bus 37 from Muiderpoort Station.*

Vliegenbos, Meeuwenlaan 138, NL-1022 AM Amsterdam, tel: 636 8855. Open 1 April–1 November. Basic camp site with 400 pitches. *Bus 32, 39 from the Centraal Station.*

Cyclist with friend

Youth hostels

The address of the Dutch Youth Hostel Association is Nederlandse Jeugdherberg Centrale (NJHC), Prof. Tulpplein 4, NL-1018 GX Amsterdam, tel: 31 20-626 4433.

There are two youth hostels in the city centre:

Stadsdoelen, Kloveniersburgwal 97, tel: 624 6832.

Vondelpark, Zandpad 5, tel: 683 1744.

There are also a number of other budget hotels for students. Two of the most popular are:

Hotel Hans Brinkers, Kerkstraat 136, tel: 622 0687.

Hotel Kabul, Warmoestraat 38–42, tel: 623 7158.

A list of other similar hotels can be obtained from the VVV offices.

For anyone in possession of a sleeping bag and in need of a good sleep, try:

Sleep-in, Mauritskade, 's-Gravensandestraat 51, tel: 694 7444.

Youth hostellers

Index